Cyril A Waters, Henry Fawcett

Explanatory Digest of Professor Fawcett's

Cyril A Waters, Henry Fawcett

Explanatory Digest of Professor Fawcett's

ISBN/EAN: 9783744645607

Printed in Europe, USA, Canada, Australia, Japan

Cover: Foto ©Andreas Hilbeck / pixelio.de

More available books at **www.hansebooks.com**

AN
EXPLANATORY DIGEST

OF

PROFESSOR FAWCETT'S "MANUAL
OF POLITICAL ECONOMY."

AN EXPLANATORY DIGEST

OF

PROFESSOR FAWCETT'S "MANUAL OF POLITICAL ECONOMY."

BY

CYRIL A. WATERS, B.A.

London:
MACMILLAN AND CO.
AND NEW YORK.
1887

[The Right of Translation is reserved.]

Cambridge:
PRINTED BY C. J. CLAY, M.A. AND SONS,
AT THE UNIVERSITY PRESS.

PREFACE.

THIS digest of the late Professor Fawcett's well-known *Manual of Political Economy* (6th edition, 1883, Macmillan & Co.) is designed mainly for the use of candidates preparing that work for examination, who, it is hoped, will find it useful as an explanatory guide to the more important principles established by the learned Professor.

PART I. PRODUCTION.

§ 1. *Definition of Political Economy.*

POLITICAL Economy is the Science which investigates the principles which regulate the production, distribution, and exchange of wealth.

Wealth may be defined to be any commodity which has an exchange value, e.g. water and air under ordinary conditions have no exchange value, for they can be obtained without labour and their supply is unlimited. But where water is supplied by artificial means, as in a town by reservoirs and pipes, it acquires an exchange value and becomes wealth.

Similarly the natural resources of a nation, as coal, iron, &c., have no exchange value unless there is a demand for them. 'The social condition of any country and the state of its civilization determine to what extent these resources may be classed as wealth.'

Money is not wealth but only the symbol thereof. It performs two functions:

I. It is a measure of value.
II. It is a medium of exchange.

The fallacy of the mercantile system (as it was called) lay in identifying money with wealth, and in believing that a nation's wealth consisted in an accumulation of the precious metals.

§ 2. *The Requisites of Production.*

All wealth is the product of man's labour employed on the products of nature. But while labouring, the labourer must be fed and maintained, and therefore some of the produce of past labour must be saved from consumption for this purpose.

Capital is this saving.

There are therefore three requisites for Production:

I. Labour.

II. The materials supplied by nature on which labour is employed.

III. Capital, which is the fund derived from past labour and reserved from consumption in order to maintain those engaged in present or future production.

§ 3. *Functions of Labour.*

The function of the labourer is to create utilities fixed and embodied in material objects.

There are two classes of Labour:

I. Productive.

II. Unproductive.

Productive Labour is that which creates utilities fixed and embodied in material objects.

Labour may be directly or indirectly productive.

Consumption is also divided into two kinds: I. Productive, II. Unproductive. Productive Consumption is that which assists in the production of fresh wealth, as e.g. the food consumed by the labourer,

And Unproductive Consumption is that which does not so assist, as e.g. the consumption of all luxuries.

§ 4. *On Capital.*

Capital, as has been said, is the result of saving, and consists of that part of wealth which is not consumed unproductively, but saved in order to assist future production. All commodities, or their equivalent money, which are consumed unproductively, are in no sense capital either in the case of a nation or an individual, e.g. if a farmer sells his crop, and spends one half of the proceeds in the payment of his labourers and the purchase of machinery, and the other half in the purchase of luxuries, only the first half is capital.

A demand for commodities is not a demand for labour, for the consumption of luxuries does nothing to assist future production, or to increase the capital of the country, and as the labourer is paid out of capital he eventually suffers, although at the first blush the wasteful and extravagant expenditure of the rich may be considered 'good for trade' and beneficial to the labourer. To the individual labourer, the immediate recipient of the money, it doubtless is so, but not to the labouring class as a whole. A thousand pounds, for instance, expended in the purchase of velvet does nothing to increase the capital of the country. The velvet is consumed and there is an end of it, but if the money were spent in draining land or in the purchase of machinery, or in assisting the construction of a railway, the capital of the country, and thereby the fund for the payment of the labourer, would be directly and indefinitely increased.

Although capital is the result of saving, yet it must be consumed in order to fulfil its functions, e.g. food is not capital unless it is eaten, nor machinery unless it is employed. Capital therefore only fulfils its functions when it is consumed in the creation of fresh wealth.

Money raised by a Government on loan, if spent productively, e.g. in starting railways, canals, irrigation works, &c. increases the capital of a nation; if spent unproductively, e.g. in purchasing munitions of war, it decreases such capital. 'Unproductive expenditure by Government of money raised on loan impoverishes a nation more than the unproductive expenditure of individuals, because no one has to pay these individuals anything when they spend their money unproductively, but when they lend it to the Government to be spent unproductively, the whole nation has annually to pay a certain penalty in consequence of the unproductive expenditure. The penalty paid is the interest, received by the lenders of the loan.'

Taxes paid out of income do not affect the labourer, taxes paid out of capital do.

Capital is of two kinds: I. Fixed, II. Circulating.

Circulating capital is such as only fulfils the functions of capital, i.e. assists in the creation of wealth, once, e.g. the food consumed by the labourer.

Fixed capital is such as performs, or is capable of performing these functions many times, e.g. Machinery, railway plant, &c.

§ 5. *Variations in the Productive Power of the three requisites of Production.*

The three requisites of Production are Land, Labour, and Capital. The productive power of these three all vary at different times and in different places under the influence of the following causes:

(*a*) The productiveness of land depends not only on its natural fertility, but also on the quantity of labour and capital required to make its produce available for consumption, i.e. on its vicinity to a market. Very fertile land is often nonproductive of wealth, because, being at a great distance from any market, the cost of transport would involve the consumption of more wealth than such land would produce by the application of labour and capital. On the other hand, even inferior land in the neighbourhood, say, of a great town, is immensely productive of wealth because its produce possesses the utility of being in, or near, the place where it is to be consumed, and the cost of transport is comparatively little.

(b) The productiveness of labour is regulated by three considerations:
    (1) The energy of the labourer.
    (2) His intelligence.
    (3) His integrity.

Energy, because he does more work than the slothful workman.

Intelligence, because he does that work more skilfully. Integrity, because he does not require to be watched, and the cost of supervision is thereby saved.

(c) The productiveness of capital is increased by the employment of skilled labour, by its application to fertile land, and by the use of machinery, which may increase the productiveness of capital from one to a hundredfold.

N.B. The productiveness of capital must be estimated by the amount of wealth created by it, not by the return to the capitalist, this being a different question altogether and belonging to that part of Political Economy which treats of the distribution of wealth.

The productiveness of labour is enormously increased
(a) By the division of labour, owing to three causes (Adam Smith's three causes).
    (1) The increase of dexterity in every particular workman.
    (2) The saving of time which is commonly lost in passing from one species of work to another.
    (3) The invention of a great number of machines

which facilitate and abridge labour, and enable one man to do the work of many.

A further advantage (adduced by Mr Babbage) of the division of labour, is the classification of labourers into skilled and unskilled. By the division of labour the skilled workman is enabled to devote his whole time and attention to that particular kind of work in which he has a special skill. If no such division existed he would have to devote some part of his time and labour to work which an unskilled workman could perform just as well, thereby greatly diminishing the wealth-producing power of his labour.

(*b*) The productiveness of labour is also increased by the combination or cooperation of labour, which is divided into

(1) Simple cooperation, when labourers combine their labour in the same way to do the same thing, e.g. in building a bridge or constructing a railway.

(2) Complex cooperation when labourers, engaged in different employments, lend their assistance to one another to effect a common object.

N.B. Division of labour is an instance of the complex cooperation of labour.

§ 6. *Production on a large and a small scale.*

The respective advantages of production on a large and on a small scale depend upon circumstances, but speaking generally, the extension of machinery makes the former more profitable than the latter, large mills for example creating more wealth and making a larger proportionate return on capital than small. Joint Stock Companies (where a number of persons combine their capital to work some concern) labour under the disadvantage that the supervision and effective control must be delegated to managers, who have not the same motive (i.e. of self interest) to exercise energy and economy, as private capitalists.

By giving the manager a pecuniary interest in the success of the concern, in the shape of a share in the profits, this objection is removed. Joint Stock Companies greatly promote the production of wealth, by combining and applying to a single object a variety of small capitals, which, if separately used, would be comparatively ineffective in promoting that end.

Large farming is more productive of wealth than small (in the case at least of corn and cattle), because the large farmer has usually more capital to invest in the purchase of machinery (whereby the productiveness of capital is indefinitely increased), because small farming involves small fields which necessitate the waste of a good deal of land in hedges, &c., and because in farming on a large scale a good deal of the cost of superintendence is saved, almost as many shepherds for instance being required to look after a flock of 400 sheep as after a flock of 800.

But small farming is more productive than large, where the personal care and attention of the farmer is incessantly required as in the culture of the Vine and in Dairy and Poultry farming.

§ 7. *On the Increase of Production.*

When land labour and capital are at their highest state of efficiency, the production of wealth can only be increased by increasing one or other of these, the three elements of production.

I. On the increase of land.

Fresh land is brought into cultivation owing to two causes,

(*a*) The introduction of agricultural improvements,

whereby what was formerly waste land is made productive, e.g. the Fens of Ely which, by being drained, have been converted from a swamp into fertile land.

(*b*) An increase of population requiring an increase of food supplies.

In the second case, such land being usually inferior to the best land already in cultivation and more expensive to work as requiring a greater quantity of capital and labour, the price of agricultural produce in order to remunerate the cultivator must rise; therefore as population advances food has a tendency to become more expensive.

This tendency however may be counteracted by the importation of food supplies from abroad, e.g. although population has immensely increased in England during the last fifty years, the price of corn has remained stationary, owing to the vast importation of that commodity from America, Russia, and other countries.

II. The increase of labour.

The increase of labour varies directly with the demand for labour, and inversely with the cost of food supplies, marriage among the labouring classes being greatly stimulated by a flourishing condition of trade and cheapness of food, higher wages being paid when trade is brisk owing to the greater demand for labour, and wages whether high or low possessing greater purchasing power when the necessaries of life are cheap.

III. The increase of Capital.

Capital, which, as has been already stated, is the third requisite of production, is the result of saving, and therefore can only be increased by increased saving. Men save for two motives:

I. As a prudent provision for the future.

II. In order to make wealth by an advantageous investment.

The ratio of the three elements of production to one another varies greatly in different countries, e.g. India has abundance of fertile land and cheap labour, but is deficient in capital.

England, on the contrary, has almost unlimited capital and plenty of cheap labour, but hardly any fertile land not already in cultivation. The West Indies and America have abundant fertile land and capital, but in the first-named, labour, owing to the emancipation of the slaves, cannot be got, and in the second it is extremely dear.

PART II. DISTRIBUTION.

§ 1. *Private Property and Socialism.*

THE distribution of wealth implies the idea of property, the rights possessed by holders of property being regulated by law and custom, and varying at different times and in different countries. The two main influences which regulate the distribution of wealth are,
  I. Competition, as in England.
  II. Custom.
The institution of private property being followed by great inequalities of wealth, various socialistic schemes have been propounded to remedy them, of all of which the root idea is that private property shall not exist, but all the wealth of the country shall be enjoyed in common. Of these schemes the most famous are those of Fourier and St Simon.

A strong distinction must be drawn between voluntary socialism when a number of individuals voluntarily combine to form a socialistic community, and involuntary, or compulsory socialism, i.e. socialism enforced by law.

Cooperation, in which the same individuals supply both the labour and capital necessary to work any business, and divide the profits in proportion to the shares contributed, is, in a modified form, an example of the former.

The poor law system which confers on every individual a right to maintenance, and free primary education, are examples of the latter.

[This chapter is somewhat unsatisfactory, for it contains no reference to the socialism of the German school of Socialists, Lassalle, Karl Marx and their successors, which, unlike the impracticable and exploded schemes of Fourier and St Simon, is an actual living force, and of which the dominant principle is the nationalisation of the land and the means of production.]

§ 2. *Classes among whom wealth is distributed.*

As all wealth is produced by Land, Labour, and Capital, so it is divided in the shape of Rent, Wages, and Profits, among those who have contributed these three necessary elements of production, that is to say, the Landowner, the Labourer, and the Capitalist.

In England these shares are usually received by different persons, but this is not necessarily the case.

The peasant proprietor, for instance, who farms his own land with his own capital, and dispenses with hired labour, contributes all three elements of production, and consequently receives the threefold reward himself.

The proportion in which rent, wages, and profits are allotted, is regulated by two considerations: I. Competition, where each party endeavours to get as much as he can, and the state of the market allows him. II. Custom, as in the case of the metayer system of agriculture abroad, and the system of fixed fees for professional men in England.

§ 3. *Rents as determined by Competition.*

Rent is the money paid for the use of land, &c. It varies in amount with the productiveness of the land, that is to say, with its natural fertility and convenience of situation.

Ricardo's Theory of Rent is, that the rent of any given piece of land equals the value of such land over that of the worst land in cultivation, which can only pay a nominal rent, as the return from it is only just sufficient to cover the expenses of cultivation, and remunerate the cultivator for his outlay of capital and labour.

Therefore the rent of any farm is equal to the difference between the net produce of such farm and the net produce of a farm which can only pay a nominal rent.

N.B. By net produce is meant the produce after deducting the cost of cultivation, in which is included a fair remuneration to the cultivator for his capital and labour.

Land which can be cultivated at a profit only on the condition that it is let at a nominal rent, is said to be on the margin of cultivation. Of course, if its productiveness is increased or diminished by any circumstance, it will in the first case be able to pay a rent—when the margin of cultivation is said to fall—or, in the second case, it will fall out of cultivation, when the margin of cultivation is said to rise.

The margin of cultivation rises and falls with the current rate of interest on money, and is therefore high where, as in Australia, the rate of interest is high, for no man will invest his money in cultivating inferior land when he could do more with the money by investing it in business.

The rent of land is increased by any circumstance (such as the introduction of machinery) which decreases the expenses of cultivation, and conversely, if the expenses of cultivation are augmented, as for instance, by an increase in the wages of agricultural labourers, the rent of land must be diminished.

With an increase in population there is an increased demand for food, and owing to the rise in prices, it becomes profitable to take into cultivation land which formerly would not repay cultivation; the margin of cultivation accordingly falls, for land which could formerly pay no rent is now able to pay a rent owing to the rise in prices, and with the fall in the margin of cultivation rents rise.

A portion of rent may usually be considered to represent a return to capital which has been spent in improving the land, as in the case of the fens of Lincolnshire and Cambridgeshire, which have been converted by drainage from worthless swamps into valuable arable land.

Rent is not an element in the cost of obtaining agricultural produce, for supposing all land made rent-free, while the demand for agricultural produce remained stationary, the same amount of land would have to be cultivated as before; but food could not be sold cheaper, for if so the person who cultivated a farm on the margin of cultivation, and before paid only a nominal rent, would have to cultivate at a loss and such land accordingly would fall out of cultivation. But this could not happen owing to the demand for food. Consequently this land would still be cultivated, and prices would be arranged so that the cultivator obtained the due reward for his capital and industry.

§ 4. *On Wages.*

That part of the Capital of a country which is devoted to the payment of wages is called the Wages Fund. The rate of wages depends upon the ratio between capital and population at any time, and is regulated by it; thus if the population increases while the amount of capital available for the payment of wages remains stationary, wages decline, and *vice versâ*.

The law is, Wages cannot generally rise or fall unless the capital or population of a country be increased or diminished. A rise in Wages even if capital increases may be checked by three causes:

(1) An increase of population.
(2) The introduction of labour-saving machines.
(3) The export of capital, for it is obvious that capital invested in foreign securities cannot be used in the payment of labour at home.

Wages vary greatly in different trades, and the following are Adam Smith's five causes which produce different rates of wages in different employments:

(1) The agreeableness or disagreeableness of the employments themselves.
(2) The easiness or cheapness, or the difficulty and expense of learning them.
(3) The constancy or inconstancy of employment in them.
(4) The small or great trust which must be reposed in those who exercise them.
(5) The probability or improbability of success in them.

(Mnemonic Rhyme.)

In every trade or business wages vary, don't you see?
As that trade or business pleasant or unpleasant still may be,
And as with ease and cheapness or with trouble and expense
Such trade or business may be learnt, and this is common sense,
Also as work is certain or uncertain in each trade
And according to the trust which in the workmen must be laid,
And finally, and this fifth cause will aptly end the verse
As the prospects of succeeding in't are bright or the reverse.

Illustrations:

Cause 1. Colliers for instance receive higher wages than carpenters because their work is dirty, dangerous, and laborious.

Cause 2. Wages are usually high in all those trades

which require a long apprenticeship and the expenditure of a considerable amount of capital before the learner is qualified to exercise them. This is the case in most kinds of skilled labour.

Cause 3. Wages are usually higher in those trades where employment is uncertain than in those where it is certain: e.g. the Builder's trade.

Cause 4. Wages are always high where great confidence must be reposed in the employé, as in the case of jewellers' assistants, and cashiers.

Cause 5. This cause only affects the professions, most trades being sufficiently easy to learn.

§ 5. *Profits.*

Profits are the share of wealth which are received by the capitalist as a reward for his abstinence in using his wealth as capital instead of spending it unproductively.

Profits are composed of the three following elements.

(1) A reward for saving, or more properly a reward for abstinence.

(2) Wages for the labour of superintendence.

(3) A compensation for the risk of loss.

The first element of profits may be always estimated in amount by the current rate of interest, that is to say the interest on such investments—as for instance in Government Stock—which are absolutely free from risk, and which involve no labour of superintendence on the part of the investor. For the second element, remuneration for the labour of superintendence is influenced by many of the same causes which affect the wages of ordinary labour, i.e. agreeableness or disagreeableness of the occupation, &c. Thirdly, profits are usually greatest in those trades in which the risk of loss is greatest.

The reward for saving or abstinence being expressed

by the current rate of interest, and this latter being always the same in the same country and at the same time, the profits of capital vary with the wages of superintendence and the risk of loss.

"When the profits realised in any business are just sufficient to give an adequate compensation for interest on capital for risk against loss and for labour of superintendence then it is said that the natural rate of profit is obtained."

This natural rate of profit is determined by the circumstances of the trade itself, the elements of risk, and labour of superintendence, varying in different trades, but in every trade profits have a tendency to gravitate to the rate of profit natural to such trade.

That this principle is true may be thus shown:—

When the profits in any trade rise above the rate of profit natural to such trade, they have a tendency to become reduced, owing to the following causes:

I. The competition of fresh capital introduced into the trade, which occasions a rise in the price of the raw material.

II. A constant increase in the supply of goods, which first equals, and then exceeds the demand.

III. A rise in wages owing to the competition for labour.

Similarly when the profits of any trade are unnaturally depressed, they have a tendency to recover, owing to the withdrawal of capital from such trade, and the diminution of the output, which at length becomes insufficient to meet the demand.

The rate of profit depends upon the cost of labour and "this is determined by comparing the wages the labourer receives with the amount of wealth produced by his labour."

Profits therefore vary inversely with the cost of labour

and if therefore the rate of profit is higher in one country A, than in another B, it must be because the cost of labour is less in the first than in the second.

"The cost of agricultural labour is measured by its cost when applied to the least fertile soil in cultivation, that is to say, that soil which only pays a nominal rent, for rent may be regarded as the sum which the farmer pays for permission to employ labour upon productive land. The more productive the land the higher of course is the rent; or in other words, the more favourable the circumstances under which agricultural labour is applied, the higher the sum which has to be paid as rent. Although agricultural labour employed on a fertile soil is more efficient, yet the former obtains no advantage from the cost of this labour being diminished, for what he would thus gain is paid away in rent."

Mr Mill analyses the cost of labour into the following elements:—

"Cost of labour, and therefore the rate of profit, is a function of three variables.

(1) The efficiency of labour.

(2) The wages of the labourer (meaning thereby the real reward of the labourer).

(3) The greater or less cost at which the articles composing that reward can be produced or purchased."

This analysis is thus explained by Prof. Fawcett:—

"If labour becomes more efficient, while the wages of the labourer and the price of food remain unaltered, the cost of labour will be diminished. If the wages of the labourer are reduced, while there is no change in the efficiency of the labourer and the price of food, the cost of labour will again be diminished. The cost of labour will also be diminished if the price of food is reduced and the amount of the labourer's wages estimated by the commodities they will purchase for him remains unchanged. If therefore the cost of labour, or in other words, the rate of profit, varies in different countries from time to time, the variations must be due to the influence of one or more of the three causes above enumerated."

This may be put more shortly thus:—

If (A) element (1) is increased, while elements (2) and (3) remain constant, profits rise: and (B) profits also rise, if elements (2) and (3) are diminished, while element (1) remains constant.

With regard to these three elements,

(1) The efficiency of labour depends upon the supply of fertile land, labour being more or less productive of wealth as it is applied to land of greater or less fertility.

(2) The remuneration of the labourer is determined by the ratio between capital and population.

(3) The cost of producing this remuneration or real reward of the labourer is indicated by the cost of producing food supplies.

§ 6. *Peasant Proprietors.*

A peasant proprietor is one who cultivates his own land (usually of limited extent) with his own labour, and supplies his own capital, and is thus at one and the same time landlord, tenant and labourer.

This is a very common tenure of land on the Continent, and also in ancient times in England, this class of producers being known as yeomen.

The disadvantages of small farming (i.e. want of capital to purchase machinery, stock, &c. and the narrow margin between gross and net profits, owing to the necessary working expenses, many of which are as great on a small as on a large farm), are only counterbalanced in the case of peasant proprietorship, owing to that 'magic of property' which converts blowing sand dunes and barren mountain tops into fertile farms.

Peasant proprietorship, although common on the Continent, does not make way in England, owing chiefly to three causes:

(1) The custom of primogeniture.

(2) The power of settlement and entail, which locks up land and prevents its coming into the market.

(3) A cumbrous and costly system of conveyancing.

Moreover in England the possession of a landed estate confers political and social prestige, and land therefore commands a fancy price, which puts it out of the reach of men of moderate capital who desire to purchase it in small quantities in order to cultivate it for profit.

The chief reasons for introducing a system of peasant proprietorship in England are

(1) It would raise the status of the agricultural labourers by converting them into a class of small yeomen or petty freeholders.

(2) It would act as a check on over-population by inspiring that class with the virtues of thrift and sobriety, and accustoming them to prudential motives, it being reasonable to suppose from the analogy of the upper classes, that having once become accustomed to a certain "standard of comfort" they would be unwilling to fall from it by encumbering themselves with large families, and would therefore, as in France, and other countries where the system of peasant proprietorship obtains, defer marrying to a much later period in life than is now usual among the working population of England.

₄ The chief objection to peasant proprietorship is not noticed by Prof. Fawcett. The peasant proprietor on account of his want of capital is forced to borrow, and often at usurious interest, and not infrequently ends in becoming the mere drudge of the moneylender who holds the mortgage of his farm. This is largely the case among the emancipated serfs of Russia, and was a potent factor in the Juden-hetze which raged there recently, most of these usurers being Jews.

§ 7. *Métayers, Cottiers and Tenant Right.*

The métayer system of land tenure (a very common tenure on the Continent, especially in Italy) is that by which the tenant pays to the landlord as rent a fixed proportion of the produce of the soil, this proportion varying in different countries, being sometimes one-half and sometimes two-thirds, the landlord usually providing in addition to the land some part of the capital required to work it, as implements, stock, machinery, &c., furnishing one or more of these according to the custom of the country.

The métayer tenure is a customary one, and the tenants practically possess fixity of tenure.

The Irish cottier tenure, which resembles the métayer system in that the tenants are peasant cultivators, tilling the ground without the aid of hired labour, differs from it in that rents are regulated not by custom, but by competition, while it differs from the English system in that this competition is one not of capitalists but of labourers, a competition, that is to say, not of more or less well-to-do farmers who will not pay a higher rent than is consistent with a reasonable return on their capital, but of "miserably poor peasants" who, having no other occupation open to them (owing to the absence of mines, manufactories &c. through the greater part of Ireland) than that of tilling the ground, are therefore willing to pay any rent for the privilege of being able to do so. These rents of course are merely nominal; the cottier is nearly always in arrears, and benefited nothing by good seasons or good cultivation, for the increased profits merely go to liquidate these arrears, the tenant thus gaining nothing either by the exercise of his own industry or the bounty of Nature.

Ulster tenant right (which received legal sanction by the Land Act of 1870) represents the sum (sometimes amounting to as much as the fee-simple of the land) paid for the good-will of the farm by the incoming to the outgoing tenant, this sum representing partly a premium for good-will, and partly compensation for unexhausted improvements.

By the Irish Land Act of 1881 a tenant can appeal to a land-court to fix his rent, and the rent so fixed cannot be changed for 15 years*.

The chief justification for interfering by legal enactment between landlord and tenant, is, that it is to the public interest that the soil should be made as productive as possible; and that the application of capital to the land on the tenant's part, which subserves this purpose, is discouraged when he does not enjoy tenant right, that is to say, when he does not possess security of tenure, and is liable to have his improvements confiscated by the landlord in the shape of increased rent.

§ 8. *National Education and other remedies for Low Wages.*

Interference by legal enactment with the rate of wages or the hours of labour must necessarily be either futile or mischievous, for if wages are raised or the hours of labour diminished, while prices remain stationary, the profits of the capitalist are curtailed; hence he will probably withdraw his capital from home industries and invest it abroad, where it is not shackled by such restrictions. The consequence of this proceeding will be that home industries will languish and the labourer will suffer. On the other hand, if prices are raised in order to compensate the capitalist for the rise in wages, the benefit received by the labourer in the shape of increased wages is merely illusory, for the purchasing power of such wages is diminished in precise proportion to the general rise in prices, and he is on the same condition as before.

* By the Irish Land Act of the present year (1887) the land-courts are now empowered to revise these rents.

This would be the effect of a general rise of wages in every employment.

In the next case, suppose that the wages of the labourers engaged in some particular employment—of agricultural labourers for example—were compulsorily raised. Owing to the fact that an increase in wages has a directly stimulating effect on population, the result would simply be that in a short space of time there would be a glut of labour in that employment, "an excess" that is to say "in the supply of labour when compared with the demand for it", which so far from improving the condition of the labourer would greatly injure it.

That the Government should be obliged to find work for the unemployed (except as a temporary expedient) is open to the objection that it would enormously stimulate population, if the labourer were always sure of obtaining employment, while, as his wages would be paid by money raised by taxation, the drain on the resources of the taxpayer would, with the increase of population, at length reach such a point as practically to exhaust them.

The real remedy for low wages (according to Prof. Fawcett) is national education, which

(1) Increases the efficiency (or wealth-producing power) of labour by increasing the intelligence of the labourer.

(2) Diminishes crime and pauperism.

(3) Exercises a prudential check on population by raising the standard of comfort of the labourer.

Other means of improving the condition of the poor, are emigration, which drains off the surplus supply of labour, cooperation, allotment gardens, &c.

§ 9. *Trades-Unions and Strikes.*

A trades-union is an organization or combination of the workmen engaged in any trade, designed partly to fulfil the ordinary functions of a friendly society, but chiefly to regulate the rate of wages in that trade, to protect the interests of the workmen, and to enable them to meet the masters on equal terms.

To keep up wages, trades-unions endeavour to artificially limit the supply of labour, e.g. by forbidding the master workmen to take more than a certain number of apprentices. This plan has the following mischievous consequences:

1. It makes manufactured articles, owing to the scarcity of labour, dearer than they would otherwise be, thus injuring the consumer.

2. It throws the labour it excludes, on to other employments, in which perhaps there is already a glut of labour.

3. It interferes with personal liberty, by interfering with the workman's natural right of choosing what trade he will adopt.

Moreover the intermeddling of trade-unions often has the effect of driving away capital from those neighbourhoods in which their influence is most powerful.

The main object of trades-unions, indeed their real *raison d'être*, is to regulate the rate of wages, and this object they effect by directing the combined workmen to go out on strike if the wages offered by the masters are not in the opinion of the directors of the union sufficiently high.

Prof. Fawcett discusses at some length the question, whether workmen by combining are able when any trade is exceptionally prosperous to obtain higher wages; which question he decides in the affirmative, for although wages like profits have a tendency to find their level in a natural average by the migration of labour from poorly paid to more highly paid occupations, yet this law, owing to various causes, requires some time to produce its effects, and in the interval the workmen in any trade enjoy a monopoly as it were of labour, and by combining, and threatening to strike, are able to force the masters to give higher wages. Strikes and lock-outs are an inevitable result of the present system, by which the masters endeavour to buy labour as cheap, and the workmen to sell it as dear, as possible. The only way to obviate these evils is to give the workmen in any business a beneficiary interest in the success of that business, by assigning them a share of the profits. This plan would in all probability be especially successful in agriculture.

§ 10. *Cooperation.*

By cooperation, is understood the case in which the persons engaged in any business, whether one productive or distributive of wealth, supply the capital as well as the labour necessary to work it, and divide the profits among themselves, as in the case of a mill, or retail shop, carried on by the employés therein.

What is usually understood by the term cooperation is not truly such, but rather a joint-stock speculation, a number of persons supplying the requisite capital and dividing the profits, but not admitting the labourers to any share in them, e.g. the London Cooperative Stores.

The most striking examples of this latter form of cooperation so called, are the Rochdale Pioneers' Society, established 1844, and the Wholesale Society, which grew out of it, established about 1860, also the London Civil Service, Army and Navy Stores &c.

The customers, both of the Rochdale Society, and of the London Stores, benefit as well as the shareholders in these concerns. The customers of the first-named receive at the end of every quarter a certain share of the profits, in proportion to the amount of their purchases, while the customers of the London Stores are able to buy their goods twenty per cent. cheaper than at the retail shops.

The secret of the success of these stores is, that they trade for ready money only, and allow no credit, by which system the following advantages are secured:

(1) No loss is incurred by bad debts, and no capital is locked up in book-credits.

(2) The maximum of business can be carried on with the minimum of capital.

(3) The managers of the stores by selling for ready money are able to give ready money for what they buy, and can thus buy in the best and cheapest market.

The chief defect of these societies is, as has been stated above, that no share in the profits is assigned to the employés.

The above are examples of cooperative distribution.

The principles of cooperation have also been applied to production, especially in the cotton trade, for example, the Sun Mill at Oldham, but with nothing like the same amount of success, and it may be decided that cooperation is more adapted to distribution than production.

Cooperation in the true sense is well adapted to agriculture, as it supplies all the advantages while avoiding the disadvantages of peasant proprietorship, the labourers having the strongest interest in making the land as productive as possible, while by clubbing their capital they are enabled to farm on a large scale.

§ 11. *State Socialism and the Nationalization of the Land.*

Prof. Fawcett contends that if the land is nationalised, i.e. made national property, it must be either with or without compensation. If without compensation such nationalisation would be mere confiscation and flagrantly unjust; but if with compensation, that is to say, payment to the landowners of the full market value of the land, the position of the tenant would not be improved, for in order to make the scheme a financial success, and avoid jobbery and corruption, a competition or rack rent would have to be charged for the use of the land, and therefore the tenant would be as badly off as before. It may be urged, in reply to this argument, that the object of those who wish to make the land national property, is not merely to benefit the cultivator, but to benefit the whole community, by bringing the rent of land which now goes into the pockets of the landowners, into the Treasury, and devoting it to Imperial purposes and the remission of taxation.

The professor himself observes that in India, by Lord Cornwallis's permanent settlement in 1793, whereby the State relinquished its proprietary rights over a large part of Bengal to the Zemindars or tax collectors for a fixed annual payment, a considerable amount has been lost which might have been devoted (for instance) to the remission of that burdensome duty, the salt tax; and similarly in Australia, if the State retained the land in its own hand, it would escape the future necessity of imposing many more or less burdensome taxes.

Prof. Fawcett admits that if the land were nationalised the cultivator "would be protected against capricious eviction and would be secured adequate compensation for any improvements that might be effected in the land through his capital and skill," but he contends that these advantages can be secured by legal enactment without having recourse to so extensive a scheme as Land Nationalisation, and he is inclined to seek the solution of the present agrarian problem in England in the repeal of the laws of primogeniture, settlement, and entail which tie up land and prevent it passing freely from owner to owner.

The chief objection to the construction of railways, canals and other public works by Government, in order to give additional employment to the labouring classes, is that if such works were a profitable investment they would be undertaken by private enterprise, and therefore where they are not so undertaken they must result in a deficit if undertaken by Government, which deficit can only be met by additional taxation.

The objection to State aided cooperation and State aided peasant proprietorship is that dependence on the community instead of dependence on one's own efforts saps the feeling of independence and its attendant virtues of sobriety, patience, industry, self-denial, &c.

If houses were built for the working classes by the State or municipality, a full competition or rack rent would have to be charged for them in order to avoid jobbery and financial failure, and even then the State or municipality would compete at a disadvantage with private enterprise, which is always more economical and efficient.

Moreover it would discourage the efforts of the working classes to build better houses for themselves through the agency of building societies, &c.

With regard to Prince Bismarck's scheme of levying a compulsory tax—say of ten per cent—on manufacturers' profits in order to provide an insurance fund for their workmen, it is certain that such tax would in the long run be paid by the workmen themselves, for as the manufacturer would be unable to raise the price of commodities owing to foreign competition, he would either withdraw his capital from home industries and invest it abroad, thereby diminishing the demand for labour, or reimburse himself by lowering the wages of his workmen, and in either case the labourer would equally suffer.

Other examples of socialism or semi-socialism are the English poor-law, and free education. Of the former the professor approves as a safeguard against the evils of indiscriminate charity, but objects to the latter that it saps the feeling of independence, by encouraging the parent to regard the education of his child as a burden which he may shift on to the shoulders of the taxpayer.

§ 12. *On the Economic Aspects of Slavery.*

The slave-owner who farms his own land, claims the entire produce, like the peasant proprietor, no part of his profits going in the payment of wages, as his slaves are mere chattels, and as much a part of his capital as his cattle or horses.

Slave-labour, according to Prof. Cairnes, is characterised by the three following capital defects:

I. It is given reluctantly.
II. It is unskilful.
III. It is wanting in versatility.

It is given reluctantly because the slave has no motive of self-interest to spur him to exertion. Whether he works ill or well he is sure to receive food, clothing and lodgement, and he is sure to receive no more however well he works.

II. It is unskilful, and III. it is wanting in versatility for the same reason, as the slave has no motive of self-interest to make him exert his mental faculties.

As slave labour is given reluctantly and requires constant supervision, slaves can only be worked in gangs, and as such labour is unskilful, and lacking in versatility, it is useless in arts and manufactures.

Therefore the only commodities to the production of which slave labour is adapted are the four following: cotton, tobacco, rice and sugar.

PART III. EXCHANGE.

§ 1. *On Value and Price.*

The *value* of any commodity is that quantity of any other commodity for which it will exchange, e.g. if a sack of wheat will exchange for a ton of coal, a ton of coal is the *value* of a sack of wheat.

Hence there cannot be a general rise in values, for value implies the comparison of one commodity with another, and one commodity can only become more valuable than others, by others becoming less so.

Price is a particular case of value, being the value of any commodity when compared with the precious metals which have been adopted as money.

Hence there *can* be a general rise in prices, prices rising as money becomes more plentiful, and falling as it becomes more scarce. Prices will also rule low if the commodities which can be purchased with money are exceptionally plentiful.

§ 2. *On the Causes which regulate the Prices of Commodities.*

The commodities which compose a nation's wealth may be divided into three classes:

I. Those of which the supply is absolutely limited, and cannot be increased by increased labour, as e. g. rare coins, pictures by deceased artists, &c.

II. Those of which the supply can be increased, but of which the additional production, by requiring a greater proportionate expenditure of labour and capital, has a tendency to become more expensive. This is particularly the case with agricultural produce.

III. Those of which the supply can be indefinitely increased without increased cost, as manufactured articles.

CLASS I. Price of Commodities of which the Supply is absolutely Limited.

The value of all commodities in this class is regulated not by the 'law of supply and demand,' which in this connection is a misleading phrase, but by an equalisation of the supply with the 'effectual demand,' the wish, that is to say, combined with the power to purchase. The law is:—

"The demand depends upon the price. The price must be such that the demand will exactly equal the supply."

Example. A, B, C are each willing to give £1000 for a picture by Turner: the demand is obviously greater than the supply. B and C are willing to give £1500 for it: the demand is still greater than the supply. C however is willing to give £2000 for the picture rather than not have it, while B will not go, say, beyond £1900. The picture therefore will be knocked down to C at some price between £1900 and £2000, determined, according to Adam Smith's expression, by the "higgling of the market," and thus the demand, which has all along been influenced by the price, is made equal with the supply. (Fawcett's illustration.)

Two elements compose the exchange value of all commodities.

I. Value in use or utility.
II. Difficulty of attainment.

No commodity, however useful it may be, has any exchange value if no difficulty is involved in its attainment, example, water; and, on the other hand, no commodity has any exchange value if it has no value in use, i. e. if it does not satisfy some want or desire. The price of commodities is usually determined by difficulty of attainment rather than value in use, but in the case of commodities falling under Class I. value in use is the determining element, but this element is not capable of satisfactory analysis, as it depends upon a complex variety of motives.

§ 3. *Causes which regulate the Price of Commodities continued.*

CLASS II. Price of Agricultural and Mineral Produce.

The chief distinction to be remembered between commodities falling under Class II. and those falling under Class III. is, that an increased demand for the former usually causes an advance in price, but this is not necessarily the case with the latter.

The cost of agricultural produce must be such as to leave the farmer a fair return on his capital after deducting the expenses of cultivation, in which are included rent, wages of labour, &c. for otherwise the farmer will withdraw his capital from farming and invest it in some other trade or pursuit.

The rent of a farm is determined by the pecuniary value of its produce over that of the worst land in cultivation, such land only paying a nominal rent.

Rent however, as explained above (page 13), forms no part of the cost of agricultural produce, for the price of such produce must always necessarily be such as to return a fair profit on his labour and capital to the farmer of the worst land in cultivation, which only pays a nominal rent. If this were not the case such land would be thrown out of cultivation, but this cannot take place owing to the demand for agricultural produce.

But although "the price of agricultural produce is not affected by the payment of rent," the reverse is true, for with an increased demand for food the margin of cultivation descends, prices rise, and as was explained in Part II. § 3 there is also a general rise in rents.

Therefore,—High prices mean high rents, but prices themselves are regulated simply by the demand for food.

Although an advancing population is the chief cause of a rise in prices, owing to the increased demand for food, which necessitates recourse to inferior land requiring a greater expenditure of labour and capital for its cultivation, yet even with an increasing population there are two causes which may prevent prices rising:

I. An increased importation of food supplies from abroad.

II. The introduction of machinery and other agricultural improvements, which economize the cost of cultivation and increase the productiveness of the soil.

The price of mineral produce is regulated by laws similar to those which regulate the price of agricultural produce. For example, if the prices quoted for coal are too low, the less productive mines will be abandoned, the low prices not affording a sufficient return for the expense incurred in working them, while, on the other hand, to meet an increased demand, recourse will be had to such mines, thereby necessitating a rise in prices to recompense the extra amount of labour and capital expended in working them, the price of coal, like the price of food, being fixed by the price of what is produced by the least productive sources of supply.

The law is, the demand varies inversely with the price, for the greater the price the less the demand; while the price varies directly with the demand, for the greater the demand the greater the price, the price being eventually such as to equalize the supply to the demand.

§ 4. *On the Causes which regulate the Price of Commodities, continued.*

CLASS III. Price of Manufactured Commodities.

The third class of commodities consists of those whose production can be indefinitely increased without increased cost. Such are manufactured articles, for as in such articles the cost of the raw material forms only a minor element in their cost, an increased demand for them, unlike an increased demand for agricultural or mineral produce, is not necessarily followed by a rise in prices, for by the use of machinery they can be turned out on a large scale not only without increased, but even with diminished cost of production.

Setting aside therefore the cost of the raw material, which is a comparatively inoperative element of the cost of manufactured produce, we find that the elements of such cost are

 I. Wages of Labour.
 II. Profits of Capital.

If either of these elements rise above the natural rate in any trade, the price of commodities manufactured in that trade also rises, and similarly their fall is accompanied by a fall in prices.

 I. If an increased demand necessitates a rise in wages, prices must also rise to recoup the manufacturer for his increased outlay.

 II. For the second element, unnaturally large profits cannot permanently be secured in any trade, the competition of capital stimulating an increased output, which will sooner or later outstrip the demand, whereupon prices will return to their natural level. Therefore

The price of manufactured articles is regulated by two principles:

I. It must on the average approximate to the cost of production, this latter term including cost of material, wages of labour, and natural profits of capital.

II. The demand (meaning 'effective demand,') for a commodity, varies inversely with its price, and the price at any particular time must be such as to equalize the demand to the supply.

The competition of capital secures the acting of the first law, and with regard to the second it is important to bear in mind that the price of any commodity *must always be such as to equalize the supply and demand.*

§ 5. *On Money.*

Money performs two functions.

I. It is a measure of value.

II. It is a medium of exchange.

Any substance selected by a community (as pressed cubes of tea by the Chinese, and cowrie-shells by certain African tribes) to serve as a medium of exchange, and obviate the necessity for barter, may be regarded as the money of that community, but by most civilized nations the precious metals have been selected to serve the purposes of money, for the following reasons:

I. As a measure of value they are subject to as few variations as possible.

II. As a medium of exchange they possess an intrinsic value, as well as great value in small bulk.

I. It is undesirable that the substance selected for the standard of value should be liable to great or sudden fluctuations, for in that case a commodity which to-day was worth such and such an amount, might a few days hence be worth fifty per cent. less or more.

Credit would thus be disturbed, and mercantile affairs thrown into confusion.

II. It is desirable that the substance selected for the medium of exchange should possess something more than a conventional value, and also that it should possess great value in small bulk, for otherwise when any large payment had to be made, the amount of money that would have to be carried to pay it, would prove an inconvenient weight.

For these reasons the precious metals have been found by experience to prove the best standard of value, as well as the best medium of exchange.

Either gold, or silver, or both, may be adopted as a standard of value. The last case is called the adoption of a double standard, or bi-metalism, and it is implied by it that payments can be made either in gold or silver at the option of the payer.

The peculiar disadvantage attaching to it is, that if either metal became depreciated in value, say if silver became depreciated to the extent of 5 per cent. owing to the market being flooded with silver from new and extremely productive mines, any debtor could liquidate his debt in the depreciated metal, thus defrauding his creditor of the full amount due to him.

The present standard in England is a single or gold one, silver not being legal tender above forty shillings, nor copper above one shilling. The silver and copper coins form in fact only a subsidiary coinage.

§ 6. *On the Value of Money.*

The expression 'value of money' has two senses—the one popular, the other scientific,—which must be carefully distinguished from one another.

What is usually meant by the term 'value of money,' is the current rate of interest, indicated by the Bank rate of discount, and thus money is said to be more or less valuable as the interest given for its use is greater or less.

But what political economists understand by the term 'value of money' is its purchasing power, i.e. its power of obtaining other commodities in exchange for itself, and thus the value of money is said to vary with its purchasing power, being low when prices are high and high when prices are low.

This statement is unaffected by the fact that the price of gold is fixed by law, that the fixed Mint price of an ounce of gold for example is always £3. 17s. 10½d., for as such gold is purchased to be minted into coin, and the authorities of the Mint know that there is sufficient amount of gold in an ounce of bullion to be coined into £3 and the fraction of a sovereign represented by 17s. 10½d., this merely means that the values of gold in bullion and of coined gold are identical. The Mint price of gold is in fact merely the value of uncoined money in coined money, and has no connection with the value of money, i.e. its purchasing power in relation to other commodities.

The value of the precious metals is regulated by the same laws as those which regulate the price of agricultural and mineral produce, that is to say, they become more valuable as the demand for them increases, owing to the necessity of working less productive sources.

The precious metals subserve two purposes.

I. They are used as an ordinary article of commerce for the manufacture of jewellery, plate, &c.

II. They are used as a standard of value and as a circulating medium, that is to say as Money.

The demand for gold as an article of commerce is very slight (comparatively) and subject to few variations, and may therefore be disregarded.

Exchange.

As a circulating medium the demand for gold depends upon two considerations.

I. It increases *cæteris paribus* with the wealth and population of the country, and also

II. With the number of times a commodity is bought and sold before it is finally consumed.

I. The amount of money in any country must bear some proportion to its wealth and population, for although the transactions of wholesale commerce are usually carried on by cheques, bills of exchange, &c., without the assistance of money, yet coined money is always required for the discharge of petty debts and small payments, such as wages of servants, cab-hire, &c., and therefore as a country grows in material wealth and populousness, it is obvious that a greater amount of money will be required for these purposes.

II. In the second case, it is obvious that a greater amount of money will be required the oftener commodities change hands before they are finally consumed, the different middlemen having to pay one another for the commodities on each transfer.

The above therefore are the causes which regulate the demand for gold. As the demand increases, gold becomes more scarce and prices fall, the value of gold, that is to say its purchasing power, varying directly with its scarcity and inversely with the price of commodities. It follows therefore that the amount of gold in a country varies directly with prices: if prices are low gold is scarce, and if prices are high, gold, it may be inferred, is plentiful.

But as gold by becoming more scarce becomes more valuable, that is to say as its purchasing power is increased by its scarcity, it becomes more profitable to supply it; the industry of mining for gold is stimulated, and an agency is called into action which has a tendency to diminish the scarcity of gold and to equalize the supply of gold to the demand. Similarly if the supply of gold is plentiful, its power of purchasing commodities is diminished, and high prices rule. Hence the industry of mining for gold becomes less profitable, and the less productive mines will be abandoned, the tendency in both cases being to equalize the supply to the demand. It is desirable that the amount of gold in circulation should increase with the increase of wealth and population, and that it should neither outstrip nor fall short of the demand, to prevent prices fluctuating.

If the supply of gold were greatly in excess of the demand or *vice versâ*, it would give rise to grave inconveniences, for in the first case the recipient of a fixed income would find the purchasing power of his income seriously diminished, owing to the general rise in prices, while in the second case, anyone who had a fixed money payment to make would virtually pay much more than the nominal amount, the purchasing power of this amount being increased in direct proportion to the fall in prices.

§ 7. *Foreign Commerce and International Trade.*

The chief advantage of Foreign Commerce, or the interchange of commodities between different countries, is, that it enables every country to devote itself to the production of those commodities in regard to which it has been especially favoured by nature, most lands possessing some natural advantages, either not shared at all or not shared in an equal degree by other countries, England for instance being especially rich in coal and iron, while France and America have a vast acreage adapted to the growth of corn and other cereals. Therefore when England takes the corn of France in exchange for her own iron, both countries are obviously benefited, while at the same time labour and capital are economized and the productiveness of both labour and capital enormously increased.

Exchange.

Before the time of Adam Smith, and the appearance of his *Wealth of Nations*, these advantages were not perceived, it being held, in accordance with the fallacious principles of the Mercantile System, that a nation's wealth or prosperity consisted in an accumulation of the precious metals, and therefore with a view to furthering this end, with a view, that is to say, to bringing money into the country and keeping it there, the exportation of commodities was encouraged by bounties, and their importation discouraged by the imposition of duties.

To secure the advantages of international trade, it is only necessary that the commodities interchanged between any two countries should bear a different relative value in the two countries, i. e. that of any two commodities, one should be relatively dearer than the other in the one country than it is in the other. For example, say that
the cost-price of 1 ton of iron in France is £30,
„ „ „ England is £10 ;
„ 1 sack of wheat in France is 30s. or £1. 10s.
„ „ „ England is £1.

Hence although iron and wheat are both dearer in France than in England, yet French iron is three times as expensive per ton as English iron, while French wheat is only one and a half times more expensive per sack than English wheat; and while one ton of iron in France costs 20 sacks of wheat, 1 ton of English iron costs only ten. Hence it is to the mutual advantage of France and England to exchange their iron and wheat.

Prof. Fawcett explains in the course of an elaborate analysis what would be the terms of exchange of any two commodities—say wheat and iron—between any two countries, say England and France. He arrives at the following results:—

I. The prices of commodities exchanged between any

two countries are regulated by the same laws as those which regulate prices in home-trade, the self-acting law which tends to equalize the supply to the demand being constantly in operation in both cases. Therefore the profits of the exporting country on the commodity it exports vary in a direct ratio with the demand of the importing country. Thus if the demand in France for English iron at a certain price, is, owing to any causes, diminished, this price must be lowered until the demand is made equal to the supply, that is to say, England will have to give more iron in exchange for the wheat it requires.

II. If the cost of producing one of the two commodities is lowered in one country but not in the other, the country in which it is diminished will not necessarily reap the advantage. Owing to the diminution of the cost of production, the supply of that commodity will be proportionately increased, but if the demand for it in the importing country was previously exactly equal to the supply, the supply will now be in excess of the demand, and the price must be reduced until the demand is made equal to the supply (the demand for any commodity it must be remembered, being stimulated by a reduction in price). This reduction will be effected by the competition of capitalists vying with one another to secure a market.

The effect of international trade is to cheapen commodities in every country which are of the same kind as those which are imported into it. Thus by the introduction of French wheat the price of English wheat declines, and similarly the price of iron in France is lowered by the importation of English iron. Thus the consumer is benefited and at the same time the producer is not injured, except perhaps temporarily, for the price of the commodity similar to the imported commodity being driven down, capital will gradually be withdrawn from its production to the production of other commodities, and thus things will in the long run right themselves, for by the competition of capital the profits in any trade are prevented from permanently rising above, or falling beneath, the rate of profit natural to that trade. The objections to free trade spring from the fact that its opponents direct their attention to the temporary injury suffered by special classes of producers by the importation of certain commodities, and overlook the general benefit secured by the whole body of producers and consumers alike.

By the doctrine of 'reciprocity' is signified conditional free trade, the admittance, that is to say, duty free of the products of other countries, if they will receive ours in a similar manner in return.

This reasoning, says Prof. Fawcett, is fallacious, for even if other countries will not take our products, it is still to our interest to purchase theirs, if we can buy them cheaper than we could produce them ourselves*.

Under a free trade system "the difference of price of any commodity in any two countries is exactly equivalent to the cost of sending this commodity from the one country to the other," i.e. to the cost of carriage. If the

---

* The Professor perhaps hardly does sufficient justice to the argument for 'reciprocity.' It may be put thus:—Imports, it is agreed, are paid for by exports, e.g. we purchase the corn we import from France by the iron we export to her. But if foreign countries refuse to take our exports, or, which is the same thing, impose a prohibition duty on them, in order to protect the native producers, how are we to go on buying commodities from them? It is plain that we can only continue to do so by drawing on capital, and this in the long run means financial collapse.

> To buy and sell is very well.
> To sell and buy we all should try.
> But if we buy and do not sell,
> R. U. I. N. that course doth spell.

But see p. 69.

price exceeds the cost of carriage, capitalists will vie with one another in exporting the commodity from the country where it is cheaper to the country where it is dearer, until the market is overstocked and prices fall to the same level in both countries.

Although the aggregate imports of every country are paid for by the aggregate exports, these need not be exactly equal, for if any country, say for example England, is the creditor of other countries for large amounts as interest on loans, if in short it has a large amount of capital invested abroad, the countries in its debt will find it to their advantage to liquidate the interest on their debt in commodities rather than in specie, and hence the imports of this particular country will permanently exceed its exports.

§ 8. *On the Transmission of the Precious Metals.*

The precious metals are transmitted from one country to another in the two following ways:—

(1) They are exported as an ordinary article of commerce from the countries which produce them, such, for instance, as Australia and California, in exchange for the imported commodities of other countries.

(2) They are transmitted as bullion or specie from one country to another in the shape of loans, interest on investments, &c., that is to say, as money.

Regarded as articles of commerce, the export and import of the precious metals are regulated by the same laws as those which regulate the international trade in other commodities, that is to say, their exchange value varies directly with the demand of the countries to which they are exported.

It is desirable, as has been explained above (p. 38), that the amount of gold and silver in circulation should keep pace with the increase of wealth and population, in order to avoid any great fluctuation in prices, as such fluctuation not only inflicts great hardship on certain classes, those for instance in receipt of fixed incomes or who have fixed payments to make, but also causes great disturbance in general commerce.

Although the amount of gold in circulation at any particular time may be generally plentiful or the reverse, it cannot long remain either the one or the other (comparatively) in any particular country. For example, if the amount of gold in England were doubled to-morrow, prices would rise in proportion; this would induce (1) the English consumer to import commodities from abroad, where they are cheaper, and (2) the foreign merchant to export commodities to England, in order to share in the rise in prices. By these means the rise in prices would be checked, owing to the drain of money sent abroad to pay for these commodities.

§ 9. *Foreign Exchanges.*

The exchange of commodities between different countries is usually carried on, not by the transmission of specie in payment for them, but by bills of exchange*, such bills being discounted (i.e. cashed for a small consideration) by a class of men known as bill discounters, or bill brokers, who in their turn exchange the bills drawn on their own country, with foreign brokers for bills drawn on foreign countries.

The following example will illustrate the nature of bills of exchange:—

---

* A bill of exchange is a written promise by one person to another that the former will pay the latter a certain sum on a specified day, it being stated in the bill what consideration has been given for the debt which has been incurred.

Mr Andrew Marvell, coal-merchant of London, sells to M. Pierre Ronsard, a merchant of Paris, a cargo of coal for £1000, Ronsard giving Marvell a bill of exchange for the amount, this bill of exchange being a written promise to pay the £1000 on a certain specified date. At the same time, Mr Edmund Waller, another English merchant, buys of M. Théophile Gautier, a silk merchant of Lyons, a cargo of silk for £1000, giving in his turn a bill of exchange for the amount. Now how shall Ronsard and Waller discharge their debts?

Some expense will be incurred by the transmission of specie from the one country to the other for this purpose, and there is also the risk of the coin being lost by shipwreck or otherwise. Obviously the most convenient course will be for Ronsard to pay the money he owes to Marvell, to Gautier, and for Waller to pay in his turn the money he owes to Gautier, to Marvell. As long as Marvell and Gautier are paid each his thousand pounds, it is a matter of indifference to them who pays them, and by the adoption of this plan no money leaves either France or England, and the risk and expense of transmitting specie are not incurred.

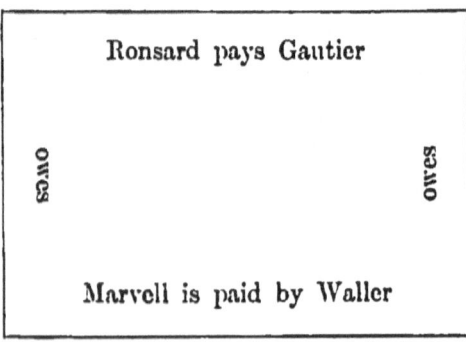

Bill discounters in France and England collect these bills drawn by one country on the other and exchange them.

When the exports and imports of a country are exactly equal to one another, the exchange is said to be at par, the bills drawn on it to pay for its imports being just equal to the bills drawn on foreign countries to pay for its exports.

But when the imports of a country exceed its exports the exchange is said to be against it, because specie must be exported to the country to which it is in debt, to liquidate that part of its debt which is not met by bills of exchange drawn on that country.

In this case the bills of exchange drawn on this foreign country will be at a premium, the merchants of the home country competing with one another to obtain them, being willing, if the cost of transmitting specie is, say, two per cent., to give even as much as one and a half per cent. premium in order to escape the necessity of transmitting specie.

Similarly the bills in the foreign country drawn on the home country will fall to a corresponding discount, for if one country, say England, has purchased of another country, say France, commodities to the amount of £12,000,000 and given bills of exchange for that amount, while it has exported to it and received bills for commodities to the amount of only £10,000,000, there are obviously £2,000,000 worth of bills drawn on England in France which cannot be exchanged for bills drawn on France in England, but must be transmitted to England and specie sent out in exchange to France. The cost of such transmission of specie being assumed to be two per cent. the French bill discounters will therefore only give £98 for a £100 bill drawn on England.

The above reasoning is based on the assumption that the currencies of the two countries are identical, but it is equally true when the two countries have different currencies, the only exception being, that in the latter case, when the exchange is against any country, the money of that country is depreciated in value relatively to the money of the country which has the exchange in its favour.

To sum up, the premium and discount on bills of exchange cannot in any case be greater than the cost of transmitting specie, their greater or less approximation to this cost being determined by the greater or less competition of merchants to obtain such bills.

§ 10. *The Functions of Credit.*

Credit signifies the relation which exists between borrower and lender, and therefore necessarily implies trust or confidence; for no one will lend to one in whose willingness and ability to repay he has no confidence.

The true definition of credit is *the power to borrow wealth*, the extent of this power in any case being indicated by the rate of interest charged for the loan, this varying inversely with the goodness of the security, i. e. with the willingness and ability of the borrower to repay.

Credit is largely concerned in the creation of wealth, for when the owner of wealth is unwilling or unable to employ it productively himself, he may by lending it to persons in whom he has confidence—that is to say, to individuals, banks, Governments, or public companies, receiving interest for the loan (such interest varying with the quality of the security)—cause it to be employed in the production of fresh wealth.

§ 11. *The Influence of Credit on Prices.*

The most common forms assumed by Credit are Bills of Exchange, Bank-notes, Cheques.

(1) A bill of exchange, as explained above (p. 43, note), is a written promise to pay a certain sum on a specified

date, which is mentioned in the bill. Such bills are transferable and can be discounted, i.e. sold for ready money by anyone who holds them, providing of course that the security is good.

It is usual for a bill of exchange to be endorsed (as it is called) by some responsible third party putting his name on the back of it, thereby binding himself to pay the sum mentioned in the bill to the party in whose favour it is drawn, if the drawer of the bill should be unable, when the time for settling it comes round, to meet his engagements. When a bill discounter cashes a bill he may also require a second endorsement by the person from whom he purchases the bill.

(2) A bank-note is a written promise given by a bank to pay a certain sum mentioned on the note at any time on demand.

By issuing notes drawn on his bank a banker is enabled to use his credit to a large extent, for it is a well-known fact that only one-third of the amount so issued need be kept in the shape of legal tender to meet ordinary emergencies, and the banker is thus enabled to use the other two-thirds for his own benefit.

N.B. I. Bank of England notes are legal tender: the notes of other banks are not. II. The Bank of England is bound to give gold in exchange for its own notes if required to do so, and hence our paper currency is said to be convertible.

Only banks founded before 1844 are allowed to issue their own notes.

(3) A cheque is a written authority, given by a person having money in a bank, to another, to draw the whole or any part of that money out.

Ex. AB gives CD a cheque on the London and Westminster for £1000, CD sends the cheque to Coutts, where he banks, and instructs them to put it to his account.

EF gives *GH* a cheque on Coutts for £1000, *GH* sends the cheque to his bankers, the London and Westminster, telling them to place it to his account. Coutts now holds a cheque on the London and Westminster for £1000, and the London and Westminster holds a cheque on Coutts for the same amount. If they exchange cheques their mutual obligation will be cancelled, and this is done through the London Clearing House, where bills of exchange and cheques change hands sometimes to the extent of £150,000,000 in a single week.

Credit is to a great extent a substitute for money, and bills of exchange, cheques and bank-notes discharge the functions of the precious metals, bills of exchange doing so in the operations of wholesale commerce, and bank-notes and cheques in the ordinary relations of life; hence the law, that if the wealth and population of a country be increased, a greater quantity of the precious metals will be required as a circulating medium, or otherwise prices would decline, may be counteracted to some extent by the employment of credit in its various forms, i.e. bills of exchange &c., these forms of credit discharging the functions of money and dispensing with the necessity for an increased supply of the precious metals. If credit did not exist and all buying and selling were carried on with ready money, it is plain that the demand for gold and silver would be enormously increased, and if an adequate supply of the precious metals were not forthcoming "a greater amount of buying and selling would have to be performed by the money already in circulation. This is equivalent to saying that general prices would rise."

In the second place, credit exerts a still more important influence on prices, by encouraging speculation and increasing the purchasing power of the country.

If merchants were compelled to pay ready money for all commodities in which they dealt, speculation would be non-existent and commerce greatly hampered, but if they are able to use their credit, their purchasing power is indefinitely increased. By buying commodities when prices are low, and giving bills for the amount, and reselling the same commodities when prices rise, and before the bills fall due, they are enabled to realise a handsome profit. Two examples are given by Prof. Fawcett of traders using their credit to make large speculative purchases of commodities, namely the speculation in tallow just before the Russian War 1854, and in tea before the war with China 1839.

This speculative use of credit has a tendency to force up prices of those commodities which are the subject of such speculation, sometimes doing so to a point far exceeding the cost of production.

Of course if merchants abuse their credit to speculate recklessly, they will be unable, when the time for settling arrives, to meet their engagements, and a commercial panic will ensue. As these panics are caused by an abuse of credit, and as bank-notes were thought to be the chief instruments of credit, the Bank Charter Act was passed in 1854 to limit the issue of bank-notes.

By the provisions of this Act the Bank of England is required to keep an equivalent amount of bullion for all the notes it issues above £14,000,000, private banks established after the passing of the Act are forbidden to issue their own notes, and those established before, only allowed to do so under certain conditions.

Whether this bank Act really fulfils the object for which it is passed, i.e. the prevention of commercial panics, is a matter of considerable controversy. Prof. Fawcett opines that it does not. The Act, he says, in ordinary times is inoperative, for prudential considerations will restrain bankers from unduly forcing the note circulation of the country; and besides, in the larger operations of commerce, bills of exchange, and not bank-notes, are really the main instruments of credit. In the later stages of speculation when the bubble bursts and a sudden shrinkage of credit ensues, the Act so far from doing good is distinctly mischievous, for it has invariably been found that whenever such a panic occurs, "credit cannot be restored without a suspension of the Act" and the anxiety as to whether, and when, the Act will be suspended, adds greatly to the dangers and difficulties of the situation.

The only remaining form of credit to be noticed is that of inconvertible bank-notes. These may either be made legal tender or not, and different results ensue in either case, but as the only paper currency in England is a convertible one, it is not necessary to consider this form of credit in detail.

§ 12. *On the Rate of Interest.*

The rate of interest is determined in this country by the interest given for money invested in the public funds or consols, which on an average of years closely approximates to three per cent.

This interest may be considered as a remuneration for saving, as an investment in consols is considered to involve no labour of superintendence and no element of risk.

The current rate of interest then, is determined by the interest on investments which entail no labour of superintendence and no risk of loss, in our country by the interest on Government Stock.

The rate of interest in any country varies with the desire of the inhabitant of that country to accumulate capital, and with the amount of capital accumulated, and also with the demand which exists for that capital. Thus if there is a great demand for capital, the rate of interest or price given for its use will be high. Saving, consequently, will be stimulated until an amount of capital is accumulated greater than the demand, when the rate of interest will fall, and saving will be checked. The rate of interest, or price of money, is regulated by the same law as that which regulates the price of other commodities, that, namely, which tends to equalise the supply with the demand.

The rate of interest is high in countries where property is insecure, and likewise in young and prosperous countries, e.g. Australia, where capital is unusually productive, owing to an abundant supply of fertile land, for when capital is unusually productive, it is obvious that those who wish to borrow it will be willing to give a larger sum for its use.

With a rise in the general rate of interest, the price of Consols and other securities, the interest on which is fixed, will decline, for it is plain that if the interest on Consols at par is 3 per cent. and 3½ or even 4 per cent. can be obtained elsewhere on good security no one will any longer be willing to give £100 for £100 worth of Consols. In the first case £100 Consols would fall to 85$, and in the second case to 75.

The price of land will also decline with a rise in the general rate of interest.

§ 13. *The Tendency of Profits to fall as a Nation advances.*

Although the rate of profit in any particular trade may be measured by a rise or fall in prices, prices rising as the demand exceeds the supply, and falling as the supply exceeds the demand, yet a *general* rise in prices can exercise no influence on the rate of profit, for such a general rise or fall merely shows that the purchasing power of gold has been increased or decreased.

The rate of profit really depends on the ratio in which whatever wealth is produced, is divided between employer and employed.

If the share received by the labourer is increased while other things remain equal, it is plain that that received by the capitalist must be decreased, and therefore the rate of profit will decline and *vice versâ*.

Prices have a tendency to decline as a nation advances in wealth and population, owing to two causes:

I. The competition of accumulated capital which tends to lower the rate of profit, until at length there comes what may be called a "glut of capital," that is to say, a time arrives when more capital has been accumulated than can be profitably invested.

II. An increase in the cost of production, caused by an increase in the cost of food, owing to the necessity of having recourse to less productive land to feed an increased population, labour as is well known being cheap when food is cheap, and *vice versâ*.

These causes which tend to lower the rate of profit, may be counteracted severally

I. By the exportation of capital and the investment thereof in foreign securities.

II. By the importation of food supplies from abroad, and by agricultural improvements, as for example, machinery, drainage, artificial manures, which cheapen food by economising labour, and increasing the productiveness of the soil.

The rate of profit may also be prevented from declining by the conversion of floating into fixed capital (thereby diminishing the wages-fund) and by commercial panics, a large amount of surplus capital being absorbed in either way.

In young countries like Australia a high rate of profit prevails, owing to the large amount of fertile land possessed by such countries, for capital is always more or less productive of wealth, as it is applied to land of greater or less fertility. In such countries the general rate of profit is regulated by the profits on agriculture, for when a man can make large profits by engaging in agriculture, he will not be induced to engage in other pursuits unless he is certain of securing profits proportionately high.

§ 14. *Over-production, or Excess of Supply.*

Although there may be temporarily over-production in any particular trade, that is to say more commodities may be produced in that trade than can be sold at remunerative prices, yet there can be no such thing as a general over-production in the sense in which that expression was understood by Malthus, Sismondi and Chalmers, the sense, namely, of more commodities being produced than can be consumed, for the demand for commodities is regulated by their price; lower the price and the demand will be indefinitely increased. Excessive production would it is true be disadvantageous to the producers, for it would imply a low rate of profit; but the commodities so produced would not be wasted; they would only be more widely distributed.

§ 15. *The Gold Discoveries.*

About the years 1848—50 the amount of gold in circulation was greatly increased by the gold discoveries in California and Australia; indeed the yield of gold was thereby immediately trebled, the previous yield of £10,000,000 per annum being raised to £30,000,000. The present section will be devoted to considering the influence on prices caused by this vast increase in the annual supply of gold.

Although such an investigation is rendered difficult by the fact that a rise or fall in prices does not furnish an accurate measure of the amount of gold in circulation, owing to the want of uniformity in such rise or fall, some commodities advancing, and others falling in price (for many other causes, as is well known, besides the value of gold affect the price of commodities) and although the inquiry is further complicated by the fact, that, owing to the speculative and as it were gambling character of goldmining, what would otherwise furnish a certain indication of a fall in the value of gold, namely the abandonment of the less productive mines, does not invariably occur (miners holding on to such mines in the hope that they may strike a new and immensely productive lode at any time), yet it may on the whole be concluded that for about twenty years after the Californian and Australian gold discoveries, there was a depreciation in the value of gold variously estimated at from 10 to 15 per cent.

Further depreciation was checked by the increased demand for gold as a circulating medium, caused by the vast expansion of international trade which coincided in point of time with the gold discoveries of Australia and America, an expansion due partly to the repeal of the navigation laws, and the system of free-trade instituted by Sir Robert Peel, partly to the extension of railways, and the application of steam as a motive-power to ships and machinery. This expansion in trade easily consumed by far the largest part of the increased yield of gold, and prevented what would otherwise have inevitably occurred, and what would have occasioned grave inconvenience, a great and sudden decline in the exchange value of gold.

The demand for gold was further stimulated by its being required to replace the very large amounts of silver sent shortly after the Indian Mutiny 1857, to India and the East to pay the labourers engaged on the construction of great public works—such as railways, &c.—organized by the Indian Government about that time; the silver thus withdrawn from the currencies of France, Germany, and other Continental countries, being replaced partly by an increased issue of gold, partly by the issue of a small paper currency.

Of late years there has been in the opinion of some political economists a decided rise in the value of gold, caused partly by a decline in the gold supply, partly by the resumption of cash payments by Italy and the United States, and partly by the demonetisation of silver and the adoption of a gold standard of value by Germany and other Continental countries, these causes tending to increase the demand for gold concurrently with the falling off in the supply.

Owing to the uncertainty attending mining for the precious metals, it would be idle to hazard a prophecy as to the value of gold in the near or distant future, but considering how possible is a great or sudden change in its value, and the grave inconvenience occasioned by such change, it would be well both for Governments and individuals not to make arrangements on the supposition that the value of gold will always remain the same as at present.

Having explained the effects produced by the discoveries of the precious metals in foreign countries, it is sufficient to state briefly that the effect produced by such discoveries in the countries in which they occur, is to raise prices and stimulate production.

Australia, which possesses extensive tracts of fertile land, lacked the other two instruments of production. These were supplied by the gold discoveries, which at one and the same time supplied capital and attracted labour, emigrants flocking to the gold fields in large numbers in the hope of making a fortune.

Not all were successful, and a large amount of this labour was ultimately diverted to agriculture and other productive employments.

§ 16. *The Depreciation in the Value of Silver.*

While gold has in all probability somewhat risen in value during the last few years, there has been on the other hand a decided fall in the value of silver.

The probable causes of this appreciation of gold have been explained in the preceding section.

The depreciation of silver is easily accounted for, by (1) an increased supply, coinciding with (2) a diminished demand.

(1) The increase in the supply of silver may be dated from the year 1870, the production of that metal rising every year until in 1875 it reached £15,000,000, nearly double the average production between the years 1852—1862. The United States of America are the chief source of this increased supply.

(2) The diminution in the demand is accounted for partly by the demonetisation of silver and the adoption of a gold currency by Germany and the Scandinavian kingdoms*, but chiefly by the remarkable falling off in the demand for silver in India, the annual import of silver in excess of the export being £15,000,000 for the eight years previous to 1867, while during the last ten years not more than £4,500,000 per annum in excess of the export has on an average been imported.

Various causes have contributed to bring about this decline in India's demand for silver, the most effective

---

* On the other hand, the resumption of cash payments by the United States, will, it is supposed, absorb, or nearly so, the amount of silver thrown on the market by the demonetisation of that metal in Germany.

Exchange.

being the great increase of late years of the Indian home charges, and the consequent increase in India's indebtedness. Hence although India's exports exceed her imports by an amount varying between £17,000,000 and £21,000,000, yet, as she is indebted to England to the extent of £15,000,000, only £4,000,000 or £5,000,000 on an average, need annually be transmitted in specie from England to India to restore the balance of trade.

This indebtedness, it may be remarked, is, for several reasons, likely to increase rather than to diminish.

The depreciation in the value of silver has hitherto been in India, entirely in comparison with gold, no decline having hitherto been observed in its purchasing power.

A decline in its purchasing power must however inevitably occur if its value compared with gold continues to decline, for every fall in the value of silver compared with gold makes it more profitable for foreigners to purchase commodities in India, where the currency is a silver one, rather than elsewhere.

For example, say that a sovereign which was formerly worth 10 rupees is now worth 12 rupees. It is obviously to the advantage of foreigners to lay out their money in the purchase of commodities in India where the silver rupee is the standard of value, rather than in countries which have a gold standard.

Similarly, it becomes less profitable for India to purchase commodities abroad, where silver is depreciated, because she has to give perhaps 60 rupees where formerly she only gave 50.

Hence India's exports will increase, while her imports will decrease. The difference will be liquidated by an increased transmission of silver, but this increased importation of silver will, if it continues, eventually cause a rise in prices. Q. E. D.

This depreciation in the value of silver is likely to

cause considerable inconvenience to the Government of India, for the most considerable part of its revenue (amounting to about £5,000,000) is contributed by the permanent Land Tax (see page 70) which is paid in the silver rupee, and the amount so contributed, though nominally the same as that contributed before the depreciation of silver, will really be less in value in exact proportion to such depreciation.

This is a serious matter for the Indian Government, for while its revenue is received in the depreciated metal, the interest on its debt, amounting (i.e. the interest) to a fixed charge of £6,000,000 annually, has to be paid in gold. India has to purchase this gold with her silver, and of course silver being depreciated in comparison with gold, she is a considerable loser by the bargain.

Various schemes have been formulated with a view to obviating the inconveniences caused by the depreciation of silver in India, for example, the adoption of a gold standard and a gold currency, of a gold standard and a silver currency, or of a double standard, but all these schemes may be shewn to be impracticable, and even if practicable they are obnoxious to the censure that they are calculated rather to aggravate than otherwise the evils they are designed to cure.

For example, a gold currency is entirely unsuited to the wants of a country like India, where the majority of the inhabitants are extremely poor, many of them never having seen even a silver coin in the course of their lives.

The objections to a double standard have been detailed on p. 35.

Other objections may be urged to the third scheme of a gold standard and a silver currency.

The moral Prof. Fawcett draws from the depreciation in the value of silver, as also from the fluctuations which have occurred in the value of gold, is that neither metal should be regarded (as silver was regarded by the authors of the Permanent Settlement) as a fixed standard of value, for at any moment extraordinarily productive mines of gold or silver may be discovered, which would immediately and greatly alter their relative value, and throw into disorder all calculations based on the assumption that their present relative value is a permanent one.

PART IV. TAXATION.

§ 1. On the General Principles of Taxation.

THE object of taxation is to raise money for the purpose of defraying the necessary expenses of Government. This is the sole object of taxation.

The following (in a necessarily abbreviated form) are Adam Smith's four Canons of Taxation, to which all taxes should conform if they are to be defended on grounds of justice and expediency.

I. Taxation should possess equality, that is to say everyone should contribute in proportion to his ability, that is, in proportion to the revenue he enjoys under the protection of the state.

II. The tax which each person is bound to pay ought to be certain and not arbitrary.

The time of payment, the manner of payment, the quantity to be paid ought all to be clear and plain to the contributor, and to every other person.

By this means alone can extortion and insolence on the part of the tax collectors be prevented.

III. Every tax ought to be levied at the time, or in the manner in which it is most likely to be convenient for the contributor to pay it, as e.g. a tax on the rent of land or houses should be made payable about quarter-day when such rent becomes due.

IV. Taxes should be so designed as to take as little as possible from the taxed above what is brought into the Treasury of the State.

These rules are thus summarised by Prof. Fawcett;

I. Taxation should possess equality.

II. There should be no uncertainty with regard to the amount to be levied.

III. The tax should be levied at the most convenient time and in the most convenient manner.

IV. The state ought to obtain as much as possible of the whole amount levied from the taxpayer.

(*Mnemonic Rhyme.*)

Equality, Convenience, Certainty—these are the virtues three
Every tax should possess if a good one, and moreover the State Treasuree
If a country's taxation's arranged on a well-matured statesmanlike plan
Should rake in the bulk of what's levied on every taxpaying man.

Adam Smith's first Canon, 'That everyone should contribute in taxes according to his ability,' has given rise to considerable discussion, for it is not easy to perceive how this end can be secured.

Two men may possess equal incomes, but if one is a bachelor, and the other a married man with a family, the latter must necessarily contribute more to the revenue of the country in proportion to his means than the former, seeing that he consumes a greater amount of taxed commodities, such as tea, spirituous liquors, &c.; and yet it has never been urged that the income tax should be so adjusted that the unmarried should contribute more than the married.

Thus no system of taxation can be devised which

would press equally on bachelors and on married men with large families, whose expenses are naturally so much greater.

The only way in which an approximation to equality can practically be secured, is to exempt the poorer classes in the state from certain special duties, as in England the possessors of incomes under £150 per annum are exempted from the income tax.

Prof. Fawcett therefore thus restates Smith's Canon:—
"The aggregate amount which each individual pays in taxes ought to be in proportion to his ability to contribute to the revenue of the state."

§ 2. *On the Income Tax.*

In connection with the income tax, a point much controverted is whether those in receipt of temporary incomes (e. g. professional men or annuitants whose source of income ceases with their death) and persons whose income is derived from permanent sources (e. g. from land or money invested in Government securities) should be taxed at the same rate or not.

It is argued that persons whose income is of a temporary or precarious nature are less able to pay the same amount of income tax than those whose income is permanent, owing to the former being compelled to put by a large portion of their income in order to make a provision for their family, a necessity which does not exist (at least in the same degree) for those whose income is derived from permanent sources.

If the income tax were a permanent and uniform charge, it may be proved by an arithmetical demonstration that no injustice would be inflicted by both classes of income being taxed at the same rate, for the tax on incomes falling under either class could be redeemed at an equal rate; while on the other hand it may also be shewn by the same method of demonstration, that if the tax is imposed for a limited and definite period, the temporary income ought to be taxed at a lower rate than the income which is permanent.

As however the income tax in this country is neither uniform, nor levied for a limited and definite period, it would be a mistake (if we rely on the arithmetical argument) to tax incomes derived from temporary and permanent sources at different rates.

Moreover, apart from the arithmetical argument, it can be shewn that to adjust the income tax on such a principle would in practice entail an endless amount of trouble and expense (owing to the difficulty involved in capitalising temporary incomes for the purposes of the tax), if indeed such a scheme is not from its inherent difficulties altogether impracticable.

It is true that a man whose income is derived from a trade or profession is less able to pay income tax than a man whose income is derived from a permanent source like land or stocks, and theoretically the tax ought to be adjusted so as to press equally on both parties, and thus conform to Adam Smith's first Canon of Taxation, but practically, as has been stated, this would be found impracticable, and the best way of remedying inequality of taxation is not by altering and tampering with any particular tax in the chimerical hope of making it press equally on all the contributors to it, but to place "the particular class which it prejudicially affects in a relatively advantageous position with regard to some other tax." (Fawcett.)

With regard to a graduated, or progressive income tax, the chief objection to it is that it is a tax on savings, and thus calculated to discourage prudence. The more a man is enabled to save and invest, the larger his income will become, but if the larger income is to be taxed at a higher rate than the smaller, the effect on habits of thrift and providence is likely to be of a very discouraging nature.

. A graduated income tax is also open to the objection that if of a very heavy character, part of it at least would probably be paid out of capital, and this part would really be contributed, not by the rich who would nominally pay it, but by the working classes who are maintained by the circulating capital of the country.

A graduated income tax is in effect "a penalty upon the accumulation of wealth," but as such wealth usually assumes the form of capital, and is mainly employed in the payment of labour, a progressive income tax that discourages the accumulation of wealth and trenches on capital, really diminishes the wages fund devoted to the support of labour.

There are two objections to the income tax of some importance.

The first is that the tax presses with undue severity on small incomes.

Incomes under £150 are exempt from the tax altogether, and a deduction of £120 is made before assessing the tax from all incomes between £150 and £400, but a person whose income is over £400 is taxed on the whole amount.

Thus a person whose income is (say) £180 per annum has to pay income tax on £30, while a person whose income is (say) £149 is exempt from the tax altogether. A person whose income is (say) £401 has to pay income tax on the whole amount, while another person whose income is (say) £395 has to pay income tax only on £275.

To rectify these anomalies, Prof. Fawcett concurs with Mr Mill in suggesting that some fixed amount, which may be regarded as sufficient to provide the bare necessaries of existence—say £100—should be exempted from taxation in all incomes, and the remainder in all incomes taxed at the same rate.

Another objection to the income tax is that all do not contribute their fair share to it, for while certain classes are unable to escape the tax—holders of Government and English Railway Stock for instance, Government officials, and officers in the army and navy, the tax, in the one case being deducted from the dividend warrants before they are forwarded, and, in the other, from the salary or pay of such officials or officers—other classes, such as traders, manufacturers and professional men, who make themselves the return of income on which the tax is assessed, frequently put their income at a much lower figure than it really is, and thus the revenue is defrauded.

Despite these disadvantages however, it is not desirable to abolish the income tax, for it presses chiefly on the rich, and is preferable to increased taxes on commodities, which would fall on the poor.

§ 3. *Taxes on Commodities and other Indirect Taxes.*

The income tax, like the assessed taxes, i.e. the taxes on dogs, carriages, &c., is an example of direct taxation, that is to say, the tax is really, as well as nominally paid, by the person on whom it is levied. When a tax is nominally paid by one person but really by another, the tax is said to be indirect. All taxes on commodities are examples of indirect taxation, for although nominally paid by the producers or importers of commodities they are really paid by the consumer, the price of such commodities being enhanced by an amount at least equal to the amount of the tax.

Tested by Adam Smith's four Canons of Taxation, (see p. 60), we find that taxes on commodities contravene the first and fourth canons, but fulfil the conditions of the second and third.

I. Taxes on commodities necessarily fail to satisfy Smith's first canon, that there should be equality of taxation, that is to say that everyone should contribute to the revenue in proportion to his ability to pay. The price of every commodity is enhanced in proportion to the tax upon it, and thus rendered dearer as much to the poor as to the rich consumers of it, nor, owing to great practical difficulties, is it usually possible to obviate this disadvantage by taxing commodities on an *ad valorem* scale, by admitting, that is to say, the inferior qualities of commodities (as of tea or tobacco) usually consumed by the poor, either duty free or at a greatly reduced rate, and increasing in proportion the tax upon the choicer qualities consumed by the rich.

II. Taxation of commodities fulfils Adam Smith's second canon, by being certain and not arbitrary, for the importer or producer of such commodities usually knows exactly what he will have to pay, and when he will have to pay it. Almost the only exception is in the case of *ad valorem* duties, it being found by experience almost impossible to foretell beforehand what amount will have to be paid in duty.

III. A tax on commodities also conforms to Smith's third canon, for the real payer of such a tax, i.e. the consumer of the commodities in question, pays the tax at the time and in the manner most convenient to him, since he pays at the time he purchases the commodities. The tax is sometimes levied on the importer or producer of a commodity at an inconvenient time, as in the case of the duty on hops which had to be paid at a certain time whether the hop-grower had sold his hops or not, but in such cases the tax is either a bad one in itself or is badly arranged.

IV. A tax on commodities usually violates Smith's

fourth canon, and this is decidedly the most serious objection to it. Indirect taxation in the shape of taxes on commodities almost always takes more money out of the pockets of the taxpayers than it brings into the treasury of the state, and this it may do in various ways.

In the first place a large army of custom-house and excise officers will have to be maintained, although this charge may be in some degree diminished by levying duties only on a few articles of which the consumption is very great, as in England on beer, wine, spirits, coffee, tea, and tobacco. But when articles very valuable and easily portable—silk, for instance, or precious stones—are taxed, smuggling can only be prevented at a great expense.

Again, a tax on commodities may cause loss by vexatious interference with some particular trade, as in the case of the Malt Tax.

It must be remembered also that the importers and producers of commodities advance the tax in the first instance, being reimbursed by the increased price they obtain from the consumer.

"But the trader is compelled to employ a portion of his capital to make this advance, and upon this capital he will expect to obtain the ordinary trade profit; this profit the consumer must return to him in addition to the amount of the tax."

For this reason a tax on manufactured goods is preferable to a tax on the raw material, for in the former case, the manufacturer being almost immediately reimbursed, the consumer is not compelled to pay this interest on capital (in the shape of an enhanced price of the goods) in addition to the tax.

With regard to a tax on exports, the idea of making the foreigners share the burden of our taxation, by taxing exported commodities, although plausible is financially unsound.

For to tax an exported commodity would be to raise its price (for those who export the commodity must have the tax returned to them in the shape of an enhanced price) but the demand for any commodity varies inversely with its price, therefore the commodity would be exported in diminished quantities; but we pay for our imports with our exports; therefore our exports also would be diminished. But diminished imports and diminished exports are symptoms of declining trade, and consequently a mode of taxation that produces such symptoms must be financially unsound. Q.E.D.

One case must be excepted, namely, when a country has a monopoly of the commodity on which it imposes an export duty, as in the case of America, which, before the Civil War, had a monopoly of cotton. If America at that time had imposed a small export duty on cotton, it would not have greatly diminished the demand, seeing that the commodity in question was a necessary of life and could not be procured elsewhere. But when any two countries are competing with one another in the production of some article of use or necessity (e.g. England and France in the production of silk) it is plain that—*cæteris paribus*—the country which can sell that commodity at the cheapest rate will easily secure the foreign market. But even a small export duty might entail the loss of this advantage and consequently the loss of the market. Such a tax in such a case would obviously be a bad one.

The only legitimate object of taxation is to obtain a revenue to defray the expenses of Government, but taxes may also be imposed—and indeed in most foreign countries are imposed—on imported commodities for the sake of protection, in order, that is to say, to foster native industries and prevent the competition of the foreigner. Such a system of protection can have none but mischievous consequences, for as was shown in the section on Foreign

Commerce and International Trade, a free interchange of commodities between any two countries is for the benefit of both, either country being thereby enabled to devote itself to the production of those commodities for the production of which it is especially favoured by nature, and thus capital and labour attain the maximum of their efficiency in the production of wealth.

Free-trade in commodities is for the benefit of the whole body of consumers, and although it may injuriously affect particular industries, even these injuries are, as a rule, temporary only and partial.

How free-trade in provisions, for instance, affects the farming interest, has been shown in the section on Foreign Commerce and International Trade.

That it is no loss to a country to import commodities is plain, if we reflect that imports are bought with exports, and that therefore a country cannot long continue to import commodities to a large extent without largely exporting them also.

Direct taxation in the shape of an income tax, and indirect taxation in the shape of taxes on commodities, have both their peculiar merits and defects, the disadvantages of an income tax for instance being that it is more or less a tax on savings, and that some classes, e.g. traders and manufacturers, are able to escape it in great part (to say nothing of its inquisitorial character); while of taxes on commodities, on the other hand, the chief inconvenience is that it is always difficult, and sometimes practically impossible, to arrange them on an *ad valorem* scale.

Both methods of taxation contravene one or more of Adam Smith's canons, and it would not be desirable for a country to adopt either as the sole mode of taxation. A judicious combination of direct with indirect taxation will usually be found to work the best.

§ 4. *The Land Tax.*

The Land Tax may be, as in England, an impost of relatively small amount levied on the proprietors of Land, or it may be, as in India, sufficiently large to be equivalent to rent, the land tax in that country being equal to a rack or competition rent, and paid by the ryots or cultivators to the state for the use of the soil. The state being thus the general landlord, there is no landlord class as in England.

When the land of any country is owned by the state in its corporate capacity in trust for the people of that country, a land tax equal in amount to a competition or rack rent for the use of land, cannot injure the cultivator, for it is no more than he would have to pay in the shape of rent if the land was in private hands, nor, unless it exceeds a rack rent, is it injurious to the consumer of agricultural produce, such produce not being rendered dearer by rent being paid to the state in the shape of a land tax instead of to private landlords (see the section on the Nationalisation of the Land).

The Tithe may be regarded as a species of land tax. Originally it amounted in value to one-tenth the produce of the soil, was paid in kind, and devoted exclusively to the maintenance of the clergy, but since the Reformation many private individuals have become tithe-proprietors, and since the Tithe Commutation Act passed in 1837, all tithe in kind has been commuted for a fixed money payment arranged on the basis of the average price of corn for the preceding seven years. Tithe is a mere rent charge on land. It is paid by the farmer, but it is considered in the rent, and if it were abolished the rent would be proportionately increased.

§ 5. *The Poor Law and its Influence on Pauperism.*

The first Poor Law, which gave every necessitous person a legal right to relief, dates from the 43rd year of Elizabeth, and continued in existence (with many serious and those generally mischievous alterations) up to the year 1832, when the new Poor Law came into operation.

Under the old or Elizabethan Poor Law "local authorities were empowered to impose a rate upon all such real property as land and houses; the able-bodied were by its provisions compelled to work as a condition of obtaining relief; the cost of maintaining able-bodied paupers was thrown upon any of their natural relations who could afford to bear the charge. The Act also provided for the annual appointment in each parish of overseers, who were responsible for the collection of rates, and the administration of relief."

In the year 1723 an Act was passed to enable local authorities to build work-houses and make admission into them a condition of receiving relief.

By means of the Elizabethan law and this amending Act, pauperism was so greatly diminished that in the middle of the last century it was hoped that it would die out altogether.

Unfortunately this belief led to a laxer administration of the old Poor Law; what were deemed its harsher features were gradually removed, and out-door relief was encouraged, the consequence being that by 1832 pauperism had risen to so great a height as to threaten national bankruptcy.

By Gilbert's Act in 1780 the work-house test had been practically annulled, the able-bodied not being compelled to accept it as a condition precedent to relief, and by East's Act in 1815 it was formally abolished altogether.

out-door relief being substituted in all cases, and the guardians being empowered to use the rates to make up deficiency in wages.

This plan of using the poors-rate as a rate in aid of wages proved very demoralizing both to the working classes and to the employers of labour; thrift and prudence on the part of the former were discouraged, and the latter were encouraged to underpay their labourers, the difference being made up out of the rates; while the evils that naturally followed were complicated by the laws of settlement, which, by forbidding the labourer to leave the place of his birth, hindered the natural flow of labour from one place to another, from places where it was not wanted to places where it was.

These evils at last rose to such a height that in 1832 a Royal Commission was appointed to investigate the working of the Poor Law. By the labours of this commission a terribly bad state of things was revealed, and in accordance with its recommendations what is known as the New Poor Law was passed, in which a return is made, roughly speaking, to the lines of the Elizabethan Poor Law, which had been so mischievously tampered with by what are known as Gilbert's and East's Acts. "By the new Act the work-house test was again revived, the plan of granting allowances in aid of wages was abolished, the appointment of paid overseers was provided for, and an official audit of accounts was secured."

The only important amendment to this Act that has since been passed, is the Union Chargeability Act, by which the area of rating is shifted to the union from the parish.

Of the various provisions of the New Poor Law, there can be no doubt that the work-house test is the most effective in discouraging pauperism, and the decline in pauperism within recent years is chiefly to be ascribed to the stringency with which this test has been applied.

§ 6. *Local Taxation.*

Taxation, it must be remembered, is of two kinds, local and imperial, the imperial taxes being levied over the whole kingdom and devoted to the common benefit of all, while the borough and county rates, which come under the head of local taxation, are levied for purely local purposes.

One great distinction between the two is to be noticed, namely, that while the revenue and expenditure of the imperial Government not only balance on the average of years, but even leave a surplus to the good, the expenditure of local authorities is considerably in excess of their income, and the deficit has to be met by the raising of loans.

"The annual local expenditure is £61,000,000, and the amount raised by local taxation is about £40,000,000." There is thus a deficit annually of £21,000,000.

This expenditure is defended on two grounds.

(1) That the money raised on loan is spent in productive works, which will ultimately repay with interest the money spent in constructing them, and

(2) That the country is growing so fast in wealth and population that this local indebtedness need not be regarded too seriously.

Neither of these grounds of defence is of much value, for in the first place, these loans are too frequently used as income instead of regarded as capital to be employed productively, and owing to the want of a proper audit it is often impossible to tell how the money is spent, and secondly it is a perfect delusion to believe that wealth and population are growing faster than local indebtedness.

The exact contrary is really the case.

Economy will not be secured until a different system of rating to that at present existing is adopted.

At present there are too many bodies empowered to

levy rates—as the Board of Health, Poor Law Guardians, Gasworks, Waterworks, &c.—and the result is inextricable confusion.

At the present time rates have a constant tendency to increase, owing to the various schemes for the public benefit—such as Free Education, Public Libraries, Public Baths, &c.—which at present are so much in favour, and all of which must ultimately be provided for out of the rates.

This increased burden of rates presses very severely upon the poor, many of whom have no money to spare for anything but the barest necessaries, and for whom it is often a hard struggle to keep out of the poor-house.

It is a well-known fact that as rates increase, pauperism increases *pari passu*. Therefore in the interest of the poorer ratepayers, it is desirable that the present extravagant expenditure of local authorities should be checked, and also that a determined opposition should be offered to the creation of fresh rates.

§ 7. *The Incidence of Local Taxation.*

All local taxation, with some trifling exceptions (e. g. market tolls, harbour dues, &c.) is levied not on personal, but real property, i. e. land and houses.

It must be carefully borne in mind that no revenue can be obtained by local bodies by means of taxes on commodities, or by any form of taxation except rates on land and buildings. From this fact may be inferred the peculiar defect and disadvantage of local taxation, namely, that the urban rates press with undue and unequal severity on the inhabitants of houses.

It is a common error that the bulk of local taxation at the present time is raised from land.

The exact contrary is really the case, and throughout the present century the amount contributed to the rates by land has been continually decreasing, while that contributed by house property has been continually increasing.

In 1814 the proportion of the rates borne by land was 69·28,
„ „ „ „ house property was 27·84;
In 1868 the per centage contributed by land was 33·20,
„ „ „ „ house property was 47·27.

Rates are always levied, not on the owners, but the occupiers of property, whether that property be in houses or land, but the incidence of the rates differs in the two cases

In the case of land, the rates although nominally paid by the tenant, really come out of the pockets of the landlord, for the rent he obtains for the use of the land is diminished in exact proportion to the amount of the rates.

Say that the rates on a given farm are £200 per annum: if these rates were abolished the tenant could afford to pay the sum they amount to in the shape of increased rent, and if he refused to do so, it is obvious that—other things being equal—the force of competition would easily enable the landlord to secure the increased rent from someone else.

In the second case, the case of urban rates on house-property, the question is somewhat complicated by the fact that there are three persons to be considered. "In the first place there is the owner of the ground on which the house stands; secondly, there is the owner of the house itself; thirdly, there is occupier or tenant of the house."

In the course of an elaborate investigation Prof.

Fawcett demonstrates that when the area of land available for building purposes is practically unlimited, the burden of the rates falls neither on the ground-landlord, nor on the landlord of the house, but on the tenant or occupier, who is unable in this case to shift the burden on to the shoulders of either of the first-named. In the case however of building sites that have the monopoly of some special advantage, say the possession of a lovely view, or, in the case of business premises, position in a central thoroughfare, the rates fall on the ground-landlord (although nominally paid by the tenant) and he alone would benefit by their remission.

The effect of rates on the prices of commodities may be briefly stated thus :—

If foreign competition were non-existent, and if the rates in all districts were uniform, any excess in rates would be shifted by the trading classes on to the consumers of commodities, for in all occupations the average rate of profit must be obtained, or men will cease to carry them on, and if an excess in rates lowers this rate of profit below its natural level, the trader must be remunerated by obtaining an increased price for his goods.

But if rates are lower in some localities than others, or if commodities are imported under a free trade system from abroad, the force of competition prevents his obtaining this enhanced price, and he is thus compelled to bear the burden of the rates.

In consequence "the trade of a district may be seriously imperilled" in the first case, and in the second, "a constant increase in the rates might ultimately jeopardise the very existence of many branches of industry in which there is a close competition between the home and foreign producer."

Local taxation sometimes presses with unjust severity on leaseholders.

A loan say of £500,000 has been contracted by a municipality for the purpose of carrying out a new system of drainage, or some other town improvement.

The repayment, with interest, is spread, say, over a period of 21 years.

During the interval the local rates are raised in proportion in order to provide for this repayment.

If a man just before the loan is contracted has taken the lease of a house for twenty-one years, he is compelled as a householder to pay his share of these enhanced rates, and then at the end of the period his landlord (who has not paid a penny) probably informs him that the property being now increased in value owing to the recent local improvements he must pay a higher rent. "Of what avail will it be for the tenant to plead that it is he and not the landlord who has paid for the drainage works and the water?"

As Professor Fawcett somewhat cynically but no doubt truly observes, "Sooner or later of course just such a rent will be charged as the house is worth."

The ratepayers have the remedy in their own hands. They may either refuse to allow these loans to be raised at all, or they should regulate strictly the manner in which they are contracted.

THE END.

MACMILLAN AND CO.'S PUBLICATIONS.

Works by the Rt. Hon. HENRY FAWCETT, F.R.S., late Professor of Political Economy at Cambridge.

MANUAL OF POLITICAL ECONOMY. Sixth Edition, revised, with a chapter "On State Socialism and the Nationalisation of the Land," and an Index. Crown 8vo. 12s.

SPEECHES ON SOME CURRENT POLITICAL QUESTIONS. 8vo. 10s. 6d.
Contents:—Indian Finance—The Birmingham League—Nine Hours Bill—Election Expenses—Women's Suffrage—Household Suffrage in Counties—Irish University Education, &c.

FREE TRADE AND PROTECTION. An Enquiry into the Causes which have retarded the general adoption of Free Trade since its Introduction into England. Sixth and Cheaper Edition. Cr. 8vo. 3s. 6d.

INDIAN FINANCE. Three Essays. With Introduction and Appendix. 8vo. 7s. 6d.

POLITICAL ECONOMY FOR BEGINNERS, WITH QUESTIONS. Sixth Edition. By MILLICENT GARRETT FAWCETT. 18mo. 2s. 6d.

ESSAYS AND LECTURES ON POLITICAL AND SOCIAL SUBJECTS. By Right Hon. HENRY FAWCETT and MILLICENT GARRETT FAWCETT. 8vo. 10s. 6d.

Works by HENRY SIDGWICK, M.A., LL.D., Knightbridge Professor of Moral Philosophy in the University of Cambridge.

THE PRINCIPLES OF POLITICAL ECONOMY. Second Edition, revised. 8vo. 16s.

THE METHODS OF ETHICS. Third Edition. 8vo. 14s.
A Supplement to the Second Edition, containing all the important Additions and Alterations in the Third Edition. Demy 8vo. 6s.

OUTLINES OF THE HISTORY OF ETHICS, for English Readers. Crown 8vo. 3s. 6d.

MACMILLAN AND CO., LONDON.

MACMILLAN AND CO.'S PUBLICATIONS.

Works by FRANCIS A. WALKER, M.A., Ph.D., Professor of Political Economy and History, Sheffield Scientific School of Yale College; late Chief of U.S. Bureau of Statistics, &c. &c.

THE WAGES QUESTION. A Treatise on Wages and the Wages Class. 8vo. 14s.

MONEY. 8vo.

MONEY IN ITS RELATION TO TRADE AND INDUSTRY. Crown 8vo. 7s. 6d.

POLITICAL ECONOMY. 8vo. 10s. 6d.

A BRIEF TEXT-BOOK OF POLITICAL ECONOMY. Crown 8vo. 6s. 6d.

LAND AND ITS RENT. Fcap. 8vo. 3s. 6d.

THE ECONOMICS OF INDUSTRY. By A. MARSHALL, M.A., Professor of Political Economy in the University of Cambridge, and MARY P. MARSHALL, late Lecturer at Newnham Hall, Cambridge. Extra fcap. 8vo. 2s. 6d.

ECONOMICS. By ALFRED MARSHALL, M.A., Professor of Political Economy in the University of Cambridge. 2 vols. 8vo.
[*In the Press.*

Works by J. E. CAIRNES, M.A., sometime Professor of Political Economy in University College, London.

POLITICAL ESSAYS. 8vo. 10s. 6d.

SOME LEADING PRINCIPLES OF POLITICAL ECONOMY NEWLY EXPOUNDED. 8vo. 14s.

By W. STANLEY JEVONS, L.L.D., M.A., F.R.S.

THE THEORY OF POLITICAL ECONOMY. Second Edition, revised, with new Preface and Appendices. 8vo. 10s. 6d.

GUIDE TO THE STUDY OF POLITICAL ECONOMY. By Dr. LUIGI COSSA, Professor of Political Economy in the University of Pavia. Translated from the Second Italian Edition. With a Preface by W. STANLEY JEVONS, F.R.S. Crown 8vo. 4s. 6d.

SPECULATIONS FROM POLITICAL ECONOMY. By C. B. CLARKE, F.R.S. Crown 8vo. 3s. 6d.

THE SILVER POUND AND ENGLAND'S MONETARY POLICY since the Restoration, together with a History of the Guinea, illustrated by contemporary documents. By the Hon. S. DANA HORTON, a Delegate of the United States to the International Monetary Conferences of 1878 and 1881. 8vo. 14s.

MACMILLAN AND CO., LONDON.

BEDFORD STREET, STRAND, LONDON, W.C.
October, 1883.

MACMILLAN & Co.'s CATALOGUE of Works in the Departments of History, Biography, Travels, Critical and Literary Essays, Politics, Political and Social Economy, Law, etc.; and Works connected with Language.

HISTORY, BIOGRAPHY, TRAVELS, &c.

ADDISON.—ESSAYS OF JOSEPH ADDISON. Chosen and edited by JOHN RICHARD GREEN, M.A., LL.D. 18mo. 4s. 6d. (Golden Treasury Series.)

AGASSIZ (LOUIS): HIS LIFE AND CORRESPONDENCE. Edited by ELIZABETH CARY AGASSIZ. 2 vols. Crown 8vo. 18s.

ALBEMARLE.—FIFTY YEARS OF MY LIFE. By GEORGE THOMAS, Earl of Albemarle. Third and Cheaper Edition. Crown 8vo. 7s. 6d.

ALFRED THE GREAT.—By THOMAS HUGHES, Q.C. Crown 8vo. 6s.

AMIEL.—THE JOURNAL INTIME OF HENRI-FREDERIC AMIEL. Translated, with an Introduction and Notes, by Mrs. HUMPHRY WARD. In 2 vols. Globe 8vo. 12s.

APPLETON.—A NILE JOURNAL. By T. G. APPLETON. Illustrated by EUGENE BENSON. Crown 8vo. 6s.

ARNOLD (MATTHEW.)—Works by MATTHEW ARNOLD, D.C.L.
ESSAYS IN CRITICISM. New Edition, Revised. Crown 8vo. 9s.
ESSAYS IN CRITICISM. Second Series. With a Preface by LORD COLERIDGE. Crown 8vo. [*In the Press.*
HIGHER SCHOOLS AND UNIVERSITIES IN GERMANY. Second Edition. Crown 8vo. 6s.
DISCOURSES IN AMERICA. Crown 8vo. 4s. 6d.

ARNOLD (T.)—THE SECOND PUNIC WAR. Being Chapters of THE HISTORY OF ROME. By the late THOMAS ARNOLD, D.D., formerly Head Master of Rugby School, and Regius Professor of Modern History in the University of Oxford. Edited, with Notes, by W. T. ARNOLD, M.A. With 8 Maps. Crown 8vo. 8s. 6d.

ARNOLD (W. T.)—THE ROMAN SYSTEM OF PROVINCIAL ADMINISTRATION TO THE ACCESSION OF CONSTANTINE THE GREAT. Being the Arnold Prize Essay for 1879. By W. T. ARNOLD, M.A., formerly Scholar of University College, Oxford. Crown 8vo. 6s.

ARNAULD (ANGELIQUE).—By FRANCIS MARTIN. Crown 8vo, 4s. 6d.

ART.—THE YEAR'S ART: A concise Epitome of all Matters relating to the Arts of Painting, Sculpture, and Architecture, which have occurred during the Year 1880, together with Information respecting the Events of the Year 1881. Compiled by MARCUS B. HUISH. Crown 8vo. 2s. 6d.
THE SAME. 1879—1880. Crown 8vo. 2s. 6d.

ARTEVELDE.—JAMES AND PHILIP VAN ARTEVELDE. By W. J. ASHLEY, B.A., late Scholar of Balliol College, Oxford. Being the Lothian Prize Essay for 1882. Crown 8vo. 6s.

ATKINSON.—AN ART TOUR TO NORTHERN CAPITALS OF EUROPE, including Descriptions of the Towns, the Museums, and other Art Treasures of Copenhagen, Christiana, Stockholm, Abo, Helsingfors, Wiborg, St. Petersburg, Moscow, and Kief. By J. BEAVINGTON ATKINSON. 8vo. 12s.

BACON (FRANCIS.)—AN ACCOUNT OF HIS LIFE AND WORKS By EDWIN A. ABBOTT, D.D., formerly Fellow of St. John's College, Cambridge. Demy 8vo. 14s.

"BACCHANTE," 1879—1882, THE CRUISE OF H.M.S.
Compiled from the Journals, Letters and Note-Books of Prince Albert Victor and Prince George of Wales. With Additions by the Rev. JOHN NEALE DALTON, Canon of Windsor. With Maps, Plans, and Illustrations. 2 vols Medium 8vo. 52s. 6d.

BAKER (SIR SAMUEL W.)—Works by Sir SAMUEL BAKER, Pacha M.A., F.R.S., F.R.G S.:—
CYPRUS AS I SAW IT IN 1879. With Frontispiece. 8vo. 12s. 6d.
ISMAILIA: A Narrative of the Expedition to Central Africa for the Suppression of the Slave Trade, organised by Ismail, Khedive of Egypt. With Portraits, Map, and numerous Illustrations. New Edition. Crown 8vo. 6s.
THE ALBERT N'YANZA, Great Basin of the Nile, and Exploration of the Nile Sources. With Maps and Illustrations. Fifth Edition. Crown 8vo. 6s.
THE NILE TRIBUTARIES OF ABYSSINIA, and the Sword Hunters of the Hamran Arabs. With Maps and Illustrations. Sixth Edition. Crown 8vo. 6s.
THE EGYPTIAN QUESTION. Being Letters to the *Times* and the *Pall Mall Gazette*. With Map. Demy 8vo. 2s.
WILD BEASTS AND THEIR WAYS IN ASIA, AFRICA, AMERICA. From 1845—1888. With Illustrations. 8vo. [*In the Press.*

BALFOUR.—THE WORKS OF FRANCIS MAITLAND BALFOUR, M.A., LL.D., F.R.S., Fellow of Trinity College, and Professor of Animal Morphology in the University of Cambridge. Edited by M. FOSTER, F.R.S., Professor of Physiology in the University of Cambridge, and ADAM SEDGWICK, M.A., Fellow and Lecturer of Trinity College, Cambridge. In 4 vols. 8vo. £6 6s.
Vol. I. Special Memoirs, Vols. II. and III. A Treatise on Comparative Embryology. Vol. IV. P tes.
*** Vols. I. and IV. may be had separately. Price £3 13s. 6d.

BANCROFT.—THE HISTORY OF THE UNITED STATES OF AMERICA, FROM THE DISCOVERY OF THE CONTINENT. By GEORGE BANCROFT. New and thoroughly Revised Edition. Six Vols. Crown 8vo. 54s.

BARKER (LADY).—Works by LADY BARKER.
A YEAR'S HOUSEKEEPING IN SOUTH AFRICA. By LADY BARKER. With Illustrations. New and Cheaper Edition. Crown 8vo. 3s. 6d.
STATION LIFE IN NEW ZEALAND. New Edition. Crown 8vo. 3s. 6d.
LETTERS TO GUY. Crown 8vo. 5s.

BARNES.—THE LIFE OF WILLIAM BARNES, Poet and Philologist. By his Daughter, LUCY BAXTER ("Leader Scott"), Hon. Member of the Academy of Fine Arts, Florence; Author of "A Nook in the Apennines," "The Renaissance in Italy," &c. Crown 8vo. 7s. 6d.

BATH.—OBSERVATIONS ON BULGARIAN AFFAIRS. By the MARQUIS OF BATH. Crown 8vo. 3s. 6d.

BAZELY.—HENRY BAZELY, THE OXFORD EVANGELIST: A Memoir. By the Rev. E. L. HICKS, M.A., Rector of Fenny Compton; Hon. Canon of Worcester; sometime Fellow and Tutor of Corpus Christi College, Oxford. With a Steel Portrait engraved by STODART. Crown 8vo. 6s. (Biographical Series.)

BECKER.—DISTURBED IRELAND, being the Letters Written during the Winter of 1880—1881. By BERNARD H. BECKER, Special Commissioner of *The Daily News*. With Route Maps. Crown 8vo. 6s.

BEESLY.—STORIES FROM THE HISTORY OF ROME. By Mrs. BEESLY. Extra fcap. 8vo. 2s. 6d.

BERLIOZ, HECTOR, AUTOBIOGRAPHY OF, Member of the Institute of France from 1803-1865; comprising his Travels in Italy, Germany, Russia, and England. Translated entire from the second Paris Edition by RACHEL (Scott Russell) HOLMES and ELEANOR HOLMES. 2 vols. Crown 8vo. 21s.

BERNARD (ST.)—THE LIFE AND TIMES OF ST. BERNARD, Abbot of Clairvaux. By J. C. MORISON, M.A. New Edition. Crown 8vo. 6s. (Biographical Series.)

BIOGRAPHICAL SKETCHES, 1852—1875. By HARRIET MARTINEAU. With four Additional Sketches, and Autobiographical Sketch. Fifth Edition. Crown 8vo. 6s. (Biographical Series.)

BLACKBURNE.—BIOGRAPHY OF THE RIGHT HON. FRANCIS BLACKBURNE, Late Lord Chancellor of Ireland. Chiefly in connection with his Public and Political Career. By his Son, EDWARD BLACKBURNE, Q.C. With Portrait engraved by JEENS. 8vo. 12s.

BLACKIE.—WHAT DOES HISTORY TEACH? Two Edinburgh Lectures. By JOHN STUART BLACKIE, Emeritus Professor of Greek in the University of Edinburgh. Globe 8vo. 2s. 6d.

BLAKE.—LIFE OF WILLIAM BLAKE. With Selections from his Poems and other Writings. Illustrated from Blake's own Works. By ALEXANDER GILCHRIST. A new and Enlarged Edition, with additional Letters, and a Memoir of the Author. Printed on hand-made paper, the Illustrations on India paper, and mounted in the text. 2 vols. Cloth elegant, gilt, with Designs after Blake by FREDERICK J. SHIELDS. Medium 8vo. £2 2s.

BLANFORD (W. T.)—GEOLOGY AND ZOOLOGY OF ABYSSINIA. By W. T. BLANFORD. 8vo. 21s.

BOLEYN, ANNE: A Chapter of English History, 1527-1536. By PAUL FRIEDMANN. 2 vols. Demy 8vo. 28s.

BONAR.—MALTHUS AND HIS WORK. By JAMES BONAR, M.A., Balliol College, Oxford. 8vo. 12s. 6d.

BOUGHTON—ABBEY.—SKETCHING RAMBLES IN HOLLAND. By G. H. BOUGHTON, A.R.A., and E. A. ABBEY. With numerous Illustrations. Fcap. 4to. 21s.

BRIMLEY.—ESSAYS. By the late GEORGE BRIMLEY, M.A., Librarian of Trinity College, Cambridge. Edited by W. G. CLARK, M.A., Fellow and Tutor of Trinity College, Cambridge. New Edition. Globe 8vo. 5s.
CONTENTS.—Tennyson's Poems—Wordsworth's Poems—Poetry and Criticism—Carlyle's Life of Sterling—"Esmond"—"Westward Ho!"—Wilson's "Noctes Ambrosianae"—Comte's "Positive Philosophy," &c.

BRONTË.—CHARLOTTE BRONTË. A Monograph. By T. WEMYSS REID. With Illustrations. Third Edition. Crown 8vo. 6s. (Biographical Series.)

BROOKE.—THE RAJA OF SARAWAK: an Account of Sir James Brooke, K.C.B., LL.D. Given chiefly through Letters or Journals. By GERTRUDE L. JACOB. With Portrait and Maps. Two Vols. 8vo. 25s.

BROWNE.—PALÆOLITHIC MAN IN NORTH-WEST MIDDLESEX: the evidence of his Existence and the Physical Conditions under which he lived in Ealing and its Neighbourhood, Illustrated by the Condition and Culture presented by certain Existing Savages. By JOHN ALLEN BROWNE, F.G.S., F.R.G.S. With Frontispiece and Eight Plates. Demy 8vo. 7s. 6d.

BRYCE.—Works by JAMES BRYCE, M.P., D.C.L., Regius Professor of Civil Law, Oxford:—
THE HOLY ROMAN EMPIRE. Eighth Edition, Revised and Enlarged. Crown 8vo. 7s. 6d.
TRANSCAUCASIA AND ARARAT: being notes of a Vacation Tour in the Autumn of 1876. With an Illustration and Map. Third Edition. Crown 8vo. 9s.
THE AMERICAN COMMONWEALTH. Three Vols. 8vo. I. National Government. II. State Government. Party System. III. Public Opinion. Illustration. Social Institutions. [*Ready in November.*

BUCKLAND.—OUR NATIONAL INSTITUTIONS. A Short Sketch for Schools. By ANNA BUCKLAND. New Edition with Glossary. 18mo. 1s.

BUCKLEY.—A HISTORY OF ENGLAND FOR BEGINNERS. By ARABELLA B. BUCKLEY, Author of "A Short History of Natural Science." With Maps. Globe 8vo. 3s.

BURGOYNE.—POLITICAL AND MILITARY EPISODES DURING THE FIRST HALF OF THE REIGN OF GEORGE III. Derived from the Life and Correspondence of the Right Hon. J. Burgoyne, Lieut.-General in his Majesty's Army, and M.P. for Preston. By E. B. DE FONBLANQUE. With Portrait, Heliotype Plate, and Maps. 8vo. 16s.

BURKE.—LETTERS, TRACTS, AND SPEECHES ON IRISH AFFAIRS. By EDMUND BURKE. Arranged and Edited by MATTHEW ARNOLD. With a Preface. Crown 8vo. 6s.

BURN.—ROMAN LITERATURE IN RELATION TO ROMAN ART. By Rev. ROBERT BURN, M.A., Author of "Rome and the Campagna," with Illustrations. 8vo, 14s.

BURY.—A HISTORY OF THE LATER ROMAN EMPIRE FROM ARCADIUS TO IRENE, A.D. 395—800. By JOHN B. BURY, Fellow of Trinity College, Dublin. 2 vols. 8vo. [*Immediately.*

CAMBRIDGE.—MEMORIALS OF CAMBRIDGE. Greatly Enlarged and partly Rewritten (1851—66). By CHARLES HENRY COOPER, F.S.A. With Seventy-four Views of the Colleges, Churches, and other Public Buildings of the University and Town, engraved on steel by J. LE KEUX, together with about Forty-five of those engraved on Copper by STORER, and a few Lithographs, with Twenty additional Etchings on Copper by ROBERT FARREN. 8vo. 3 vols. £3 15s. Fifty copies of the Etchings, by R. FARREN, from the "Memorials of Cambridge," proofs signed in portfolio. £3 3s.

CAMERON.—OUR FUTURE HIGHWAY. By V. LOVETT CAMERON. C.B., Commander, R.N. With Illustrations. 2 vols. Crown 8vo. 21s.

CAMPBELL.—LOG-LETTERS FROM THE "CHALLENGER" By LORD GEORGE CAMPBELL. With Map. Seventh and Cheaper Edition. Crown 8vo. 6s.

CAMPBELL.—MY CIRCULAR NOTES; Extracts from Journals; Letters sent Home: Geological and other Notes, written while Travelling Westwards round the World, from July 6th, 1874, to July 6th, 1875. By J. F. CAMPBELL, Author of "Frost and Fire." Cheaper Issue. Crown 8vo. 6s.

CARLES.—LIFE IN COREA. By W. R. CARLES, F.R.G.S., H.M. Vice-Consul at Shanghai, and formerly H.M. Vice-Consul in Corea. With numerous Illustrations. 8vo. 12s. 6d.

CARLYLE.—CARLYLE PERSONALLY AND IN HIS WRITINGS. Two Lectures by DAVID MASSON, M.A., LL.D. Extra fcap. 8vo. 2s. 6d.
EARLY LETTERS OF THOMAS CARLYLE. Edited by CHARLES ELIOT NORTON. 2 vols. Vol. I. 1814-1821; 1821-1826. With two portraits. Crown 8vo. 18s.
LETTERS OF THOMAS CARLYLE. 1826—1836. Edited by CHARLES ELIOT NORTON. 2 vols. Crown 8vo. [*Immediately.*
CORRESPONDENCE BETWEEN GOETHE AND CARLYLE. Edited by CHARLES ELIOT NORTON. Crown 8vo. 9s.
REMINISCENCES BY THOMAS CARLYLE. Edited by CHARLES ELIOT NORTON. A New Edition. 2 vols. Crown 8vo. 12s.

CARPENTER.—THE LIFE AND WORK OF MARY CARPENTER. By J. ESTLIN CARPENTER, M.A. With Steel Portrait. Crown 8vo. 6s. (Biographical Series.)

CARR (J. COMYNS).—PAPERS ON ART. By J. COMYNS CARR. Extra Crown 8vo. 8s. 6d.

CARSTARES.—WILLIAM CARSTARES: a Character and Career of the Revolutionary Epoch (1649—1715). By ROBERT STORY, Minister of Rosneath. 8vo. 12s.

CASSEL.—MANUAL OF JEWISH HISTORY AND LITERATURE, preceded by a Brief Summary of Bible History, by Dr. D. CASSEL. Translated by Mrs. HENRY LUCAS. Fcap. 8vo. 2s. 6d.

CAUCASUS, NOTES ON THE. By WANDERER. 8vo. 9s.

CHATTERTON: A BIOGRAPHICAL STUDY. By DANIEL WILSON, LL.D., Professor of History and English Literature in University College, Toronto. Crown 8vo. 6s. 6d.

CHATTERTON: A STORY OF THE YEAR 1770. By Professor MASSON, LL.D. Crown 8vo. 5s.

CHURCH (R. W.)—COLLECTED EDITION OF DEAN CHURCH'S MISCELLANEOUS WRITINGS. Uniform with the Collected Works of Ralph Waldo Emerson, &c. In Five Volumes. Globe 8vo. 5s. each.
Vol. I. MISCELLANEOUS ESSAYS. | Vol IV. SPENSER.
Vol. II. DANTE and other Essays. | Vol. V. BACON.
Vol. III. ST. ANSELM.

HISTORY, BIOGRAPHY, TRAVELS, ETC.

CICERO.—THE LIFE AND LETTERS OF MARCUS TULLIUS CICERO: being a New Translation of the Letters included in Mr. Watson's Selection. With Historical and Critical Notes, by Rev. G. E. JEANS, M.A., Fellow of Hertford College, Oxford, late Assistant-Master in Haileybury College. Second Edition, revised. Crown 8vo. 10s. 6d.

CLARK.—MEMORIALS FROM JOURNALS AND LETTERS OF SAMUEL CLARK, M.A., formerly Principal of the National Society's Training College, Battersea. Edited with Introduction by his WIFE. With Portrait. Crown 8vo. 7s. 6d.

CLASSICAL WRITERS.—Edited by JOHN RICHARD GREEN. Fcap. 8vo. Price 1s. 6d. each.
EURIPIDES. By Professor MAHAFFY.
MILTON. By the Rev. STOPFORD A. BROOKE.
LIVY. By the Rev. W. W. CAPES, M.A.
VERGIL. By Professor NETTLESHIP, M.A.
SOPHOCLES. By Professor L. CAMPBELL, M.A.
DEMOSTHENES. By Professor S. H. BUTCHER, M.A.
TACITUS. By Rev. A. J. CHURCH, M.A., and W. J. BRODRIBB, M.A.
Other Volumes to follow.

CLIFFORD (W. K.)—LECTURES AND ESSAYS. Edited by LESLIE STEPHEN and FREDERICK POLLOCK, with Introduction by F. POLLOCK. Two Portraits. 2 vols. 8vo. 25s.
Popular Edition. With Portrait. Crown 8vo. 8s. 6d.

CLOUGH.—THE WORKS OF ARTHUR HUGH CLOUGH. In 2 vols. Crown 8vo, 7s. 6d. each.
I. POEMS. New and Revised Edition. II. PROSE REMAINS. With a Selection from his Letters and a Memoir. Edited by his Wife.

COOK.—A POPULAR HANDBOOK TO THE NATIONAL GALLERY. By EDWRD T. COOK, with a Preface by JOHN RUSKIN, LL.D., and Selections from his Writings. Crown 8vo. Cloth, 12s. 6d.; half Morocco, 14s.
*** Also an Edition on large paper, limited to 250 copies. 2 vols. 8vo.

COMBE.—THE LIFE OF GEORGE COMBE, Author of "The Constitution of Man." By CHARLES GIBBON. With Three Portraits engraved by JEENS. Two Vols. 8vo. 32s.

COPE.—THE ORIGIN OF THE FITTEST: ESSAYS ON EVOLUTION. By EDWARD COPE, A.M., PH.D., Member of the United States National Academy of Sciences, &c. Demy 8vo. 12s. 6d.

CORNWALL, AN UNSENTIMENTAL JOURNEY THROUGH. By the Author of "John Halifax, Gentleman." With numerous Illustrations by C. NAPIER HEMY. Medium 4to. 12s. 6d.

COUES.—NORTH AMERICAN BIRDS, KEY TO. Containing a Concise Account of every Species of Living and Fossil Bird at present known from the Continent north of the Mexican and United States Boundary, inclusive of Greenland. Second Edition, revised to date, and entirely rewritten. With which are incorporated GENERAL ORNITHOLOGY, an Outline of the Structure and Classification of Birds; and FIELD ORNITHOLOGY, a Manual of Collecting, Preparing, and Preserving Birds. By ELLIOTT COUES, M.A., M.D., Ph.D., Member of the National Academy of Science, &c. &c. Profusely Illustrated. Demy 8vo. £2 2s.

COX (G. V.)—RECOLLECTIONS OF OXFORD. By G. V. Cox, M.A., New College, late Esquire Bedel and Coroner in the University of Oxford. Cheaper Edition. Crown 8vo. 6s.

CUNYNGHAME (SIR A. T.)—MY COMMAND IN SOUTH AFRICA. 1874—1878. Comprising Experiences of Travel in the Colonies of South Africa and the Independent States. By Sir ARTHUR THURLOW CUNYNGHAME. G.C.B., then Lieutenant-Governor and Commander of the Forces in South Africa. Third Edition. 8vo. 12s. 6d.

"DAILY NEWS."—THE DAILY NEWS' CORRESPONDENCE of the War between Russia and Turkey, to the fall of Kars. Including the letters of Mr. Archibald Forbes, Mr. J. E. McGahan, and other Special Correspondents in Europe and Asia. Second Edition, Enlarged. Cheaper Edition. Crown 8vo. 6s.
FROM THE FALL OF KARS TO THE CONCLUSION OF PEACE. Cheaper Edition. Crown 8vo. 6s.

DARWIN.—CHARLES DARWIN: MEMORIAL NOTICES RE-PRINTED FROM "NATURE." By THOMAS H HUXLEY, F.R.S.; G. J. ROMANES, F.R.S.; ARCHIBALD GEIKIE, F.R.S; and W. T. THISELTON DYER, F.R.S. With a Portrait engraved by C. H. JEENS. Crown 8vo. 2s. 6d. *Nature Series.*

DAWSON.—AUSTRALIAN ABORIGINES. The Language and Customs of Several Tribes of Aborigines in the Western District of Victoria, Australia. By JAMES DAWSON. Small 4to. 14s.

DEAK.—FRANCIS DEAK, HUNGARIAN STATESMAN: A Memoir With a Preface, by the Right Hon. M. E. GRANT DUFF, M.P. With Portrait. 8vo. 12s. 6d.

DENISON.—A HISTORY OF CAVALRY FROM THE EARLIEST TIMES. With Lessons for the Future. By Lieut.-Colonel GEORGE DENISON, Commanding the Governor-General's Body Guard, Canada, Author of "Modern Cavalry." With Maps and Plans. 8vo. 18s.

DE VERE.—ESSAYS CHIEFLY ON POETRY. By AUBREY DE VERE. 2 vols. Globe 8vo. 12s.
Vol. I. CRITICISMS ON CERTAIN POETS.
Vol. II. ESSAYS LITERARY AND ETHICAL.

DE WINT.—THE LIFE OF PETER DE WINT. By WALTER ARMSTRONG, B.A. Illustrated with Twenty-four Photogravures from the Artist's Pictures. Medium 4to. 31s 6d.

DICKENS'S DICTIONARY OF PARIS, 1885.—(Fourth Year.) An Unconventional Handbook. With Maps, Plans, &c. 18mo. Paper Cover, 1s. Cloth, 1s 6d

DICKENS'S DICTIONARY OF LONDON, 1888.—(Tenth Year.) An Unconventional Handbook. With Maps, Plans, &c. 18mo. Paper Cover, 1s. Cloth, 1s. 6d.

DICKENS'S DICTIONARY OF THE THAMES, 1888.—An Unconventional Handbook. With Maps, Plans, &c. Paper Cover, 1s. Cloth, 1s. 6d.

DICKENS'S DICTIONARY OF THE UNIVERSITY OF OXFORD. 18mo. paper cover. 1s.

DICKENS'S DICTIONARY OF THE UNIVERSITY OF CAMBRIDGE. 18mo. paper cover. 1s.

DICKENS'S DICTIONARY OF THE UNIVERSITIES OF OXFORD AND CAMBRIDGE. 18mo. cloth. 2s. 6d.

DILKE.—GREATER BRITAIN. A Record of Travel in English-speaking Countries during 1866—67. (America, Australia, India.) By the Right Hon. Sir CHARLES WENTWORTH DILKE, M.P. Eighth Edition, with Additions. Crown 8vo. 6s.

DILETTANTI SOCIETY'S PUBLICATIONS. IONA, ANTIQUITIES OF. Vols. I. II. and III. £2 2s. each, or £5 5s. the set.
AN INVESTIGATION OF THE PRINCIPLES OF ATHENIAN ARCHITECTURE; or, The Results of a recent Survey conducted chiefly with reference to the Optical refinements exhibited in the construction of the Ancient Buildings at Athens By FRANCIS CRANMER PENROSE, Archt., M.A., &c. Illustrated by numerous Engravings. £7 7s.
SPECIMENS OF ANCIENT SCULPTURE; Egyptian, Etruscan, Greek, and Roman. Selected from different Collections in Great Britain by the Society of Dilettanti. Vol. II. £5 5s.
ANTIQUITIES OF IONIA. Part IV. Folio, half-morocco. £3 13s. 6d.

DOLET.—ETIENNE DOLET: the Martyr of the Renaissance. A Biography. With a Biographical Appendix, containing a Descriptive Catalogue of the Books written, printed, or edited by Dolet. By RICHARD COPLEY CHRISTIE, Lincoln College, Oxford, Chancellor of the Diocese of Manchester. With Illustrations. 8vo. 18s.

DOYLE.—HISTORY OF AMERICA. By J. A. DOYLE. With Maps. 18mo. 4s. 6d. [*Historical Course.*

DRUMMOND OF HAWTHORNDEN : THE STORY OF HIS LIFE AND WRITINGS. By Professor MASSON. With Portrait and Vignette engraved by C. H. JEENS. Crown 8vo. 10s. 6d.

HISTORY, BIOGRAPHY, TRAVELS, ETC. 7

DUFF.—Works by the Right Hon. M. E. Grant Duff.
NOTES OF AN INDIAN JOURNEY. With Map. 8vo. 10s. 6d.
MISCELLANIES, POLITICAL AND LITERARY. 8vo. 10s. 6d.

EADIE.—LIFE OF JOHN EADIE, D.D., LL.D. By James Brown, D.D., Author of "The Life of a Scottish Probationer." With Portrait. Second Edition. Crown 8vo. 7s. 6d.

EGYPT.—RECENSEMENT GÉNÉRAL DE L'EGYPTE, 15 Gamad Akhar 1299. 3 Mai, 1882. Direction du Recensement ministère de l'Intérieur. Tome premier. Royal 4to. £2 2s.

ELLIOTT.—LIFE OF HENRY VENN ELLIOTT, of Brighton. By Josiah Bateman, M.A. With Portrait, engraved by Jeens. Third and Cheaper Edition. Extra fcap. 8vo. 6s.

EMERSON.—THE LIFE OF RALPH WALDO EMERSON. By J. L. CABOT, his Literary Executor. 2 vols. Crown 8vo. 18s.

EMERSON.—THE COLLECTED WORKS OF RALPH WALDO EMERSON. (Uniform with the Eversley Edition of Charles Kingsley's Novels.) Globe 8vo. Price 5s. each volume.

1. MISCELLANIES. With an Introductory Essay by John Morley.
2. ESSAYS.
3. POEMS.
4. ENGLISH TRAITS; and REPRESENTATIVE MEN.
5. CONDUCT OF LIFE: and SOCIETY and SOLITUDE.
6. LETTERS; AND SOCIAL AIMS, &c.

ENGLISH ILLUSTRATED MAGAZINE, THE. Profusely Illustrated. Published Monthly. Number I., October 1883. Price Sixpence.

Yearly Volume, 1883-1884, consisting of 792 closely-printed pages, and containing 428 Woodcut Illustrations of various sizes. Bound in extra cloth, coloured edges. Royal 8vo. 7s. 6d.

Yearly Volume, 1884-1885, consisting of 840 closely printed pages, and containing nearly 500 Woodcut Illustrations of various sizes. Bound in extra cloth, coloured edges. Royal 8vo. 8s.

Yearly Volume, 1885-1886, consisting of 832 closely printed pages, and containing upwards of 400 Woodcut Illustrations of various sizes. Bound in extra cloth, coloured edges. Royal 8vo. 8s.

Yearly Volume, 1886-1887, consisting of 822 closely printed pages, and containing nearly 400 Woodcut Illustrations of various sizes. Bound in extra cloth, coloured edges. Royal 8vo. 8s.

Yearly Volume, 1887-1888, consisting of 832 closely printed pages, and containing nearly 500 Illustrations of various sizes. Bound in extra cloth, coloured edges. Royal 8vo. 8s.

Cloth Covers for binding Volumes, 1s. 6d. each.

ENGLISH ILLUSTRATED MAGAZINE. PROOF IMPRESSIONS OF ENGRAVINGS ORIGINALLY PUBLISHED IN "THE ENGLISH ILLUSTRATED MAGAZINE," 1884. In Portfolio. 4to. 21s.

ENGLISH MEN OF LETTERS.—Edited by John Morley. A Series of Short Books to tell people what is best worth knowing as to the Life, Character, and Works of some of the great English Writers. In Crown 8vo. price 2s. 6d. each.

I. DR. JOHNSON. By Leslie Stephen.
II. SIR WALTER SCOTT. By R. H. Hutton.
III. GIBBON. By J. Cotter Morison.
IV. SHELLEY. By J. A. Symonds.
V. HUME. By Thomas H. Huxley, F.R.S.
VI. GOLDSMITH. By William Black.
VII. DEFOE. By W. Minto.
VIII. BURNS. By Principal Shairp.
IX. SPENSER. By the Very Rev. the Dean of St. Paul's.
X. THACKERAY. By Anthony Trollope.
XI. BURKE. By John Morley.
XII. MILTON. By Mark Pattison.
XIII. HAWTHORNE. By Henry James.
XIV. SOUTHEY. By Professor Dowden.
XV. BUNYAN. By J. A. Froude.

ENGLISH MEN OF LETTERS—*continued.*

XVI. CHAUCER. By Professor A. W. WARD.
XVII. COWPER. By GOLDWIN SMITH.
XVIII. POPE. By LESLIE STEPHEN.
XIX. BYRON. By Professor NICHOL.
XX. LOCKE. By Professor FOWLER.
XXI. WORDSWORTH. By F. W. H. MYERS.
XXII. DRYDEN. By G. SAINTSBURY.
XXIII. LANDOR. By SIDNEY COLVIN.
XXIV. DE QUINCEY. By Professor MASSON.
XXV. CHARLES LAMB. By Rev. ALFRED AINGER.
XXVI. BENTLEY. By Professor R. C. JEBB.
XXVII. DICKENS. By Professor A. W. WARD
XXVIII. GRAY. By EDMUND GOSSE.
XXIX. SWIFT. By LESLIE STEPHEN.
XXX. STERNE. By H. D. TRAILL.
XXXI. MACAULAY. By J. COTTER MORISON.
XXXII. FIELDING. By AUSTIN DOBSON.
XXXIII. SHERIDAN. By Mrs. OLIPHANT.
XXXIV. ADDISON. By W. J. COURTHOPE.
XXXV. BACON. By the Very Rev. the DEAN OF ST. PAUL'S.
XXXVI. COLERIDGE. By H. D. TRAILL.
XXXVII. SIR PHILIP SIDNEY. By J. ADDINGTON SYMONDS.
XXXVIII. KEATS. By SIDNEY COLVIN.

In Preparation :—

ADAM SMITH. By LEONARD H. COURTNEY, M.P.
BERKELEY. By THOMAS H. HUXLEY.

Other Volumes to follow.

Popular Edition. One Shilling each.

ENGLISH MEN OF LETTERS. Edited by JOHN MORLEY. Now publishing Monthly. Vols. I. to XXI. [ready. Paper covers, 1s. each; cloth binding, 1s. 6d.

JOHNSON. By LESLIE STEPHEN.
SCOTT. By R. H. HUTTON.
GIBBON. By J. COTTER MORISON.
HUME. By T. H. HUXLEY, F.R.S.
GOLDSMITH. By WM. BLACK.
SHELLEY. By J. A. SYMONDS.
DEFOE. By W. MINTO.
BURNS. By Principal SHAIRP.
SPENSER. By the Very Rev. R. W. CHURCH, Dean of St. Paul's.
THACKERAY. By ANTHONY TROLLOPE.
BURKE. By JOHN MORLEY.
MILTON. By MARK PATTISON.
HAWTHORNE. By HENRY JAMES.
BUNYAN. By J. A. FROUDE.
SOUTHEY. By Professor DOWDEN.
CHAUCER. By A. W. WARD.
COWPER. By GOLDWIN SMITH.
POPE. By LESLIE STEPHEN.
BYRON. By Professor NICHOL.
DRYDEN. Bo GEORGE SAINTSBURY.
LOCKE. By THOMAS FOWLER.

⁂ And the rest of the series month by month in due course.

ENGLISH POETS : SELECTIONS, with Critical Introductions by various Writers, and a General Introduction by MATTHEW ARNOLD, Edited by T. H. WARD, M.A., late Fellow of Brasenose College, Oxford. 4 vols. Crown 8vo. 7s. 6d. each.

Vol. I. CHAUCER to DONNE.
Vol. II. BEN JONSON to DRYDEN.
Vol. III. ADDISON to BLAKE.
Vol. IV. WORDSWORTH to ROSSETTI.

HISTORY, BIOGRAPHY, TRAVELS, ETC.

TWELVE ENGLISH STATESMEN.—Under the above title Messrs. MACMILLAN and Co. are publishing a series of short biographies, not designed to be a complete roll of famous statesmen, but to present in historic order the lives and work of those leading actors in our affairs who by their direct influence have left an abiding mark on the policy, the institutions, and the position of Great Britain among states.

The following list of subjects is the result of careful selection. The great movements of national history are made to follow one another in a connected course, and the series is intended to form a continuous narrative of English freedom, order, and power.

 WILLIAM THE CONQUEROR. By EDWARD A. FREEMAN, D.C.L., LL.D.   [*Ready*.
 HENRY II. By Mrs. J. R. GREEN.   [*Ready*.
 EDWARD I. By F. YORK POWELL.
 HENRY VII. By J. GAIRDNER.
 CARDINAL WOLSEY. By Prof. M. CREIGHTON.   [*Ready*.
 ELIZABETH. By the DEAN OF ST. PAUL'S.
 OLIVER CROMWELL. By FREDERIC HARRISON.
 WILLIAM III. By H. D. TRAILL.   [*Ready*.
 WALPOLE. By JOHN MORLEY.   [*In the press*.
 CHATHAM. By JOHN MORLEY.
 PITT. By JOHN MORLEY.
 PEEL. By J. R. THURSFIELD.

ETON COLLEGE, HISTORY OF. By H. C. MAXWELL LYTE, M.A. With numerous Illustrations by Professor DELAMOTTE. Coloured Plates, and a Steel Portrait of the Founder, engraved by C. H. JEENS. New and Cheaper Issue, with Corrections. Medium 8vo. Cloth elegant. 21s.

EUROPEAN HISTORY, Narrated in a Series of Historical Selections from the best Authorities. Edited and arranged by E. M. SEWELL, and C. M. YONGE. First Series, Crown 8vo. 6s.; Second Series, 1088-1228. Third Edition. Crown 8vo. 6s.

FAY.—MUSIC-STUDY IN GERMANY. From the Home Correspondence of AMY FAY, with a Preface by Sir GEORGE GROVE, D.C.L., Director of the Royal College of Music. Crown 8vo. 4s. 6d.

FINCK.—ROMANTIC LOVE AND PERSONAL BEAUTY: Their Development, Causal Relation, Historic and National Peculiarities. By HENRY T. FINCK. 2 vols. Crown 8vo. 18s.

FISKE.—EXCURSIONS OF AN EVOLUTIONIST. By JOHN FISKE, M.A., LL.B., formerly Lecturer on Philosophy at Harvard University. Crown 8vo. 7s. 6d.

FISON AND HOWITT.—KAMILAROI AND KURNAI GROUP. Marriage and Relationship, and Marriage by Elopement, drawn chiefly from the usage of the Australian Aborigines. Also THE KURNAI TRIBE, their Customs in Peace and War. By LORIMER FISON, M.A., and A. W. HOWITT, F.G.S., with an Introduction by LEWIS H. MORGAN, LL.D., Author of "System of Consanguinity," "Ancient Society," &c. Demy 8vo. 15s.

FITZGERALD.—THE WORKS OF EDWARD. With a Memoir. Edited by W. ALDIS WRIGHT, M.A., Vice-master of Trinity College, Cambridge. 3 vols. Crown 8vo.   [*Immediately*.

FORBES (ARCHIBALD).—SOUVENIRS OF SOME CONTINENTS. By ARCHIBALD FORBES, LL.D. Crown 8vo. 6s.

FRAMJI.—HISTORY OF THE PARSIS: Including their Manners, Customs, Religion, and Present Position. By DOSABHAI FRAMJI KARAKA, Presidency Magistrate and Chairman of Her Majesty's Bench of Justice, Bombay, Fellow of the Bombay University, Member Bombay Branch of the Royal Asiatic Society, &c. 2 vols. With Illustrations. Medium 8vo. 36s.

FRANCIS OF ASSISI. By Mrs. OLIPHANT. New Edition. Crown 8vo. 6s. (Biographical Series.)

FRASER.—THE LIFE OF JAMES FRASER, Second Bishop of Manchester. A Memoir. 1818-1885. By THOMAS HUGHES, Q.C. 8vo. 16s. Popular Edition. Crown 8vo. 6s.

FREEMAN.—Works by EDWARD A. FREEMAN, D.C.L., LL.D., Regius Professor of Modern History in the University of Oxford:—

THE OFFICE OF THE HISTORICAL PROFESSOR. An Inaugural Lecture, read in the Museum at Oxford, October 15, 1884. Crown 8vo. 2s.

THE GROWTH OF THE ENGLISH CONSTITUTION FROM THE EARLIEST TIMES. Fourth Edition. Crown 8vo. 5s.

HISTORICAL ESSAYS. Fourth Edition. 8vo. 10s. 6d. CONTENTS:—I. "The Mythical and Romantic Elements in Early English History;" II. "The Continuity of English History;" III. "The Relations between the Crowns of England and Scotland;" IV. "St. Thomas of Canterbury and his Biographers;" V. "The Reign of Edward the Third;" VI. "The Holy Roman Empire;" VII. "The Franks and the Gauls;" VIII. "The Early Sieges of Paris;" IX. "Frederick the First, King of Italy;" X. "The Emperor Frederick the Second;" XI. "Charles the Bold;" XII. "Presidential Government."

HISTORICAL ESSAYS. Second Series. Second Edition, Enlarged. 8vo. 10s. 6d. The principal Essays are:—"Ancient Greece and Mediæval Italy:" "Mr. Gladstone's Homer and the Homeric Ages:" "The Historians of Athens:" "The Athenian Democracy:" "Alexander the Great;" "Greece during the Macedonian Period:" "Mommsen's History of Rome;" "Lucius Cornelius Sulla;" "The Flavian Cæsars."

HISTORICAL ESSAYS. Third Series. 8vo. 12s. CONTENTS:—"First Impressions of Rome." "The Illyrian Emperors and their Land." "Augusta Treverorum." "The Goths of Ravenna." "Race and Language." "The Byzantine Empire." "First Impressions of Athens." "Mediæval and Modern Greece." "The Southern Slaves." "Sicilian Cycles." "The Normans at Palermo."

COMPARATIVE POLITICS.—Lectures at the Royal Institution. To which is added the "Unity of History," the Rede Lecture at Cambridge, 1872. 8vo. 14s.

HISTORICAL AND ARCHITECTURAL SKETCHES: chiefly Italian. With Illustrations by the Author. Crown 8vo. 10s. 6d.

SUBJECT AND NEIGHBOUR LANDS OF VENICE. Being a Companion Volume to "Historical and Architectural Sketches." With Illustrations. Crown 8vo. 10s. 6d.

ENGLISH TOWNS AND DISTRICTS. A Series of Addresses and Essays. With Illustrations and Map. 8vo. 14s.

OLD ENGLISH HISTORY. With Five Coloured Maps. New Edition. Extra fcap. 8vo. 6s.

HISTORY OF THE CATHEDRAL CHURCH OF WELLS, as illustrating the History of the Cathedral Churches of the Old Foundation. Crown 8vo. 3s. 6d.

GENERAL SKETCH OF EUROPEAN HISTORY. Being Vol. I. of a Historical Course for Schools, edited by E. A. FREEMAN. New Edition, enlarged with Maps, Chronological Table, Index, &c. 18mo. 3s. 6d.

DISESTABLISHMENT AND DISENDOWMENT: WHAT ARE THEY? Popular Edition. Crown 8vo. 1s.

GREATER GREECE AND GREATER BRITAIN: GEORGE WASHINGTON, THE EXPANDER OF ENGLAND. Two Lectures. With an Appendix on Imperial Federation. Crown 8vo. 3s. 6d.

THE METHODS OF HISTORICAL STUDY. Eight Lectures. Read in the University of Oxford in Michaelmas Term, 1884; with the Inaugural Lecture "in the Office of the Historical Professor." 8vo. 10s. 6d.

THE CHIEF PERIODS OF ROMAN HISTORY. Six Lectures read in the University of Oxford in Trinity term, 1885. With an Essay on Greek cities under Roman rule. Demy 8vo. 10s. 6d.

FOUR OXFORD LECTURES. 1887.—Fifty Years of European History—Teutonic Conquest in Gaul and Britain. Demy 8vo. 5s.

GALTON.—Works by FRANCIS GALTON, F.R.S.:

METEOROGRAPHICA; or, Methods of Mapping the Weather. Illustrated by upwards of 600 Printed and Lithographed Diagrams. 4to. 9s.

ENGLISH MEN OF SCIENCE: Their Nature and Nurture. 8vo. 8s. 6d.

INQUIRIES INTO HUMAN FACULTY AND ITS DEVELOPMENT. With Illustrations and Coloured and Plain Plates. Demy 8vo. 16s.

RECORD OF FAMILY FACULTIES. Consisting of Tabular Forms and Directions for Entering Data, with an Explanatory Preface. 4to. 2s. 6d.

HISTORY, BIOGRAPHY, TRAVELS, ETC.

GALTON—*continued.*
LIFE HISTORY ALBUM; Being a Personal Note-book, combining the chief advantages of a Diary, Photograph Album, a Register of Height, Weight, and other Anthropometrical Observations, and a Record of Illnesses. Containing Tabular Forms, Charts, and Explanations especially designed for popular use. Prepared by the direction of the Collective Investigation Committee of the British Medical Association, and Edited by FRANCIS GALTON, F.R.S., Chairman of the Life History Sub-Committee. 4to. 3s. 6d. Or, with Cards of Wools for Testing Colour Vision. 4s. 6d.
NATURAL INHERITANCE. With Illustrations and Diagrams. 8vo.
  [*Immediately.*

GARDNER.—SAMOS AND SAMIAN COINS. By PERCY GARDNER, M.A., F.S.A., British Museum, Disney Professor of Archæology in the University of Cambridge, and Hon. Foreign Secretary of the Numismatic Society. Demy 8vo. 7s. 6d.

GEDDES.—THE PROBLEM OF THE HOMERIC POEMS. By W. D. GEDDES, LL.D., Professor of Greek in the University of Aberdeen. 8vo. 14s.

GEIKIE.—Works by ARCHIBALD GEIKIE, LL.D., F.R.S., Director-General of the Geological Survey of the United Kingdom, and Director of the Museum of Practical Geology, London, formerly Murchison Professor of Geology and Mineralogy in the University of Edinburgh, &c.
GEOLOGICAL SKETCHES AT HOME AND ABROAD. With illustrations. 8vo. 10s. 6d.
THE SCENERY OF SCOTLAND Viewed in connection with its Physical Geology. With numerous Illustrations. Crown 8vo. 12s. 6d.

GILBERT.—THE LIFE OF ELIZABETH GILBERT; and Her Work for the Blind. By FRANCES MARTIN, Author of "Angelique Arnauld." With Portrait. Crown 8vo. 6s. (Biographical Series.)

GLADSTONE.—HOMERIC SYNCHRONISM. An inquiry into the Time and Place of Homer. By the Right Hon. W. E. GLADSTONE, M.P. Crown 8vo. 6s.

GOETHE AND MENDELSSOHN (1821—1831). Translated from the German of Dr. KARL MENDELSSOHN, Son of the Composer, by M. E. VON GLEHN. From the Private Diaries and Home Letters of Mendelssohn, with Poems and Letters of Goethe never before printed. Also with two New and Original Portraits, Fac-similes, and Appendix of Twenty Letters hitherto unpublished. Second Edition, enlarged. Crown 8vo. 5s.

GOETHE.—A LIFE OF GOETHE. By HEINRICH DÜNTZER. Translated by T. W. LYSTER, Assistant Librarian National Library of Ireland. With Illustrations. Two vols. Crown 8vo. 21s.

GOLDSMID.—TELEGRAPH AND TRAVEL. A Narrative of the Formation and Development of Telegraphic Communication between England and India, under the orders of Her Majesty's Government, with incidental Notices of the Countries traversed by the Lines. By Colonel Sir FREDERICK GOLDSMID, C.B., K.C.S.I., late Director of the Government Indo-European Telegraph. With numerous Illustrations and Maps. 8vo. 21s.

GORDON.—LAST LETTERS FROM EGYPT, to which are added Letters from the Cape. By LADY DUFF GORDON. With a Memoir by her Daughter, Mrs. Ross, and Portrait engraved by JEENS. Second Edition. Crown 8vo. 9s.

GORDON (GENERAL CHARLES GEORGE). A SKETCH. By REGINALD H. BARNES, Vicar of Heavitree, and CHARLES E. BROWN, Major R.A. With Facsimile Letter. Crown 8vo. 1s.
LETTERS OF GENERAL C. G. GORDON TO HIS SISTER, M. A. GORDON. Fourth and Popular Edition. Crown 8vo. 3s. 6d.

GOSSE.—A HISTORY OF ENGLISH LITERATURE IN THE EIGHTEENTH CENTURY. By EDMUND GOSSE, Clark Lecturer on English Literature in the University of Cambridge: Editor of "The Works of Thomas Gray." Crown 8vo. [*Immediately.*

GOW.—A COMPANION TO THE CLASSICS. By JAMES GOW, M.A., Litt.D., Master of the High School, Nottingham, late Fellow of Trinity College, Cambridge. With Ill. strations. Crown 8vo. 6s.

GRAHAM.—KING JAMES I. An Historical Tragedy. By DAVID GRAHAM, Author of "Robert the Bruce." Globe 8vo. 7s.

GREAT CHRISTIANS OF FRANCE: ST. LOUIS and CALVIN. By M. Guizot, Member of the Institute of France. Crown 8vo. 6s. (Biographical Series.)

GREEN.—Works by JOHN RICHARD GREEN, M.A., LL.D.:—
THE MAKING OF ENGLAND. With Maps. Demy 8vo. 16s.
THE CONQUEST OF ENGLAND. With Maps. Demy 8vo. 18s.
HISTORY OF THE ENGLISH PEOPLE. Vol. I.—Early England—Foreign Kings—The Charter—The Parliament. With 8 Coloured Maps. 8vo. 16s. Vol. II.—The Monarchy, 1461—1540: The Restoration, 1540—1603. 8vo. 16s. Vol. III.—Puritan England, 1603—1660; The Revolution, 1660—1688. With 4 Maps. 8vo. 16s. Vol. IV.—The Revolution, 1683—1760;•Modern England, 1760—1815. With Maps and Index. 8vo. 16s.
A SHORT HISTORY OF THE ENGLISH PEOPLE. With Coloured Maps, Genealogical Tables, and Chronological Annals. New Edition, thoroughly Revised. Crown 8vo. 8s. 6d. 135th Thousand.
STRAY STUDIES FROM ENGLAND AND ITALY. Crown 8vo. 8s. 6d. Containing: Lambeth and the Archbishops—The Florence of Dante—Venice and Rome—Early History of Oxford—The District Visitor—Capri—Hotels in the Clouds—Sketches in Sunshine, &c.
READINGS FROM ENGLISH HISTORY. Selected and Edited by JOHN RICHARD GREEN. In Three Parts. Fcap. 8vo. 1s. 6d. each. Part I.—From Hengist to Cressy. Part II.—From Cressy to Cromwell. Part III.—From Cromwell to Balaklava.

GROVE.—A DICTIONARY OF MUSIC AND MUSICIANS (A.D. 1450—1886). By Eminent Writers, English and Foreign. With Illustrations and Woodcuts. Edited by Sir GEORGE GROVE, D.C.L., Director of the Royal College of Music. 8vo. Parts I. to XIV., XIX—XXI. 3s. 6d. each. Parts XV. and XVI. 7s. Parts XVII. and XVIII. 7s.
Vols. I., II., and III. 8vo. 21s. each.
Vol. I. A to Impromptu.—Vol. II. Improperia to Plain Song.—Vol. III. Planche to Sumer is Icumen In.
Cloth cases for binding Vols. I., II., and III. 1s. each.
*** Part XXII. completes the DICTIONARY of MUSIC and MUSICIANS as originally contemplated; but an Appendix and a Full General Index are in the Press.

GUEST.—LECTURES ON THE HISTORY OF ENGLAND. By M. J. GUEST. With Maps. Crown 8vo. 6s.
GUEST.—ORIGINES CELTICAE (a Fragment) and other Contributions to the History of Britain. By EDWIN GUEST, LL.D., D.C.L., F.R.S., late Master of Gonville and Caius College, Cambridge. With Maps, Plans, and a Portrait engraved on Steel by G. J. STODART. Two vols. Demy 8vo. 32s.

HAMERTON.—Works by P. G. HAMERTON:—
ETCHINGS AND ETCHERS. Third Edition, revised, with Forty-eight new Plates. Columbier 8vo.
THE INTELLECTUAL LIFE. With a Portrait of Leonardo da Vinci, etched by LEOPOLD FLAMENG. Second Edition. Crown 8vo. 10s. 6d.
THOUGHTS ABOUT ART. New Edition, revised, with an Introduction. Crown 8vo. 8s. 6d.
HUMAN INTERCOURSE. Third Thousand. Crown 8vo. 8s. 6d.

HANDEL.—THE LIFE OF GEORGE FREDERICK HANDEL. By W. S. ROCKSTRO, Author of "A History of Music for Young Students." With an Introductory Notice by Sir GEORGE GROVE, D.C.L. With a Portrait. Crown 8vo. 10s. 6d.

HARRISON.—THE CHOICE OF BOOKS; and other Literary Pieces. By FREDERIC HARRISON. Third Edition. Globe 8vo. 6s.
A Choice Edition on large paper, 250 copies only printed. 8vo. 15s.

HARPER.—THE METAPHYSICS OF THE SCHOOL. By THOMAS HARPER, (S.J.) (In 5 vols.) Vols. I. and II. 8vo. 18s. each.—Vol. III., Part I. 12s.

HEINE.—A TRIP TO THE BROCKEN. By HEINRICH HEINE. Translated by R. MCLINTOCK. Crown 8vo. 3s 6d.

HISTORY, BIOGRAPHY, TRAVELS, ETC.

HELLENIC STUDIES—JOURNAL OF. 8vo. Parts I. and II., constituting Vol. I, with 4to. Atlas of Illustrations, 30s. Vol. II., with 4to. Atlas of Illustrations, 30s., or in Two Parts, 15s. each. Vol. III., Two Parts, with 4to Atlas of Illustrations, 15s. each. Vol. IV., Two Parts, with 4to. Atlas of Illustrations. Part I. 11s. Part II., 15s. Vol. V., Two Parts, with Illustrations, 15s. each. Vol. VI., Two Part I, 15s. each. Vol. VII., Two Parts, 15s. each. Vol. VIII., Part I., 15s.
The Journal will be sold at a reduced price to Libraries wishing to subscribe, but official application must be made in each case to the Council. Information on this point, and upon the conditions of Membership, may be obtained on application to the Hon. Secretary, Mr. George Macmillan, 29, Bedford Street, Covent Garden.

HERODOTOS.—BOOKS I. TO III.—THE ANCIENT EMPIRES OF THE EAST. Edited, with Notes, Introductions, and Appendices, by A. H. SAYCE, M.A. Oxford, Hon. LL.D. Dublin; Deputy-Professor of Comparative Philology. 8vo. 16s.

HERTEL.—OVERPRESSURE IN HIGH SCHOOLS IN DENMARK. By Dr. HERTEL, Municipal Medical Officer, Copenhagen. Translated from the Danish by C. GODFREY SÖRENSEN. With Introduction by Sir J. CRICHTON-BROWNE, M.D., LL.D., F.R.S. Crown 8vo. 3s. 6d.

HILL (O.)—Works by OCTAVIA HILL.
OUR COMMON LAND. and other Essays. Extra fcap. 8vo. 3s. 6d.
HOMES OF THE LONDON POOR. Sewed. Crown 8vo. 1s.

HOBART.—ESSAYS AND MISCELLANEOUS WRITINGS OF VERE HENRY, LORD HOBART. With a Biographical Sketch. Edited by MARY, LADY HOBART. 2 vols. Demy 8vo. 25s.

HODGSON.—MEMOIR OF REV. FRANCIS HODGSON, B.D., Scholar, Poet, and Divine. By his son, the Rev. JAMES T. HODGSON, M.A. Containing numerous Letters from Lord Byron and others. With Portrait engraved by JEENS. Two vols. Crown 8vo. 18s.

HOLE.—A GENEALOGICAL STEMMA OF THE KINGS OF ENGLAND AND FRANCE. By the Rev. C. HOLE, M.A., Trinity College, Cambridge. On Sheet, 1s.
A BRIEF BIOGRAPHICAL DICTIONARY. Compiled and Arranged by the Rev. CHARLES HOLE, M.A. Second Edition. 18mo. 4s. 6d.

HOOKER AND BALL.—MOROCCO AND THE GREAT ATLAS. Journal of a Tour in. By Sir JOSEPH D. HOOKER, K.C.S.I., C.B., F.R.S., &c., and JOHN BALL, F.R.S. With an Appendix, including a Sketch of the Geology of Morocco, by G. MAW, F.L.S., F.G.S. With Illustrations and Map. 8vo. 21s.

HOZIER (H. M.)—Works by Lieut.-Col. HENRY M. HOZIER, late Assistant Military Secretary to Lord Napier of Magdala:—
THE SEVEN WEEKS' WAR; Its Antecedents and Incidents. New and Cheaper Edition. With New Preface, Maps, and Plans. Crown 8vo. 6s.
THE INVASIONS OF ENGLAND: a History of the Past, with Lessons for the Future. Two Vols. 8vo. 28s.

HÜBNER.—A RAMBLE ROUND THE WORLD IN 1871. By M. LE BARON HÜBNER, formerly Ambassador and Minister. Translated by LADY HERBERT. New and Cheaper Edition. With numerous Illustrations. Crown 8vo. 6s.

HUGHES.—Works by THOMAS HUGHES, Q.C., Author of "Tom Brown's School Days."
MEMOIR OF A BROTHER. With Portrait of GEORGE HUGHES, after WATTS, Engraved by JEENS. Sixth Edition. Crown 8vo. 5s.
ALFRED THE GREAT. Crown 8vo. 6s.
MEMOIR OF DANIEL MACMILLAN. With Portrait after LOWES DICKINSON, Engraved by JEENS. Fifth Thousand. Crown 8vo. 4s. 6d.—POPULAR EDITION. 1s.
RUGBY, TENNESSEE. Being some account of the Settlement founded on the Cumberland Plateau by the Board of Aid to Land Ownership. With a report on the Soils of the Plateau by the Hon. F. W. KILLEBREW, A.M., Ph.D., Commissioner for Agriculture for the State of Tennessee. Crown 8vo. 4s. 6d.
GONE TO TEXAS: Letters from Our Boys. Edited by THOMAS HUGHES. Crown 8vo. 4s. 6d.
THE LIFE OF JAMES FRASER. Second Bishop of Manchester. A Memoir. 1818—1885. 8vo. 16s. Popular Edition, Crown 8vo. 6s.

HUNT.—HISTORY OF ITALY. By the Rev. W. HUNT, M.A. Being the Fourth Volume of the Historical Course for Schools. Edited by EDWARD A. FREEMAN, D.C.L. New Edition, with Coloured Maps. 18mo. 3s. 6d.

HUNT.—THE PRE RAPHAELITE BROTHERHOOD. By W. HOLMAN HUNT. Illustrated by Reproductions from some of Mr. Holman Hunt's Drawings and Paintings. Crown 8vo. [*Immediately.*

HUTTON.—Works by R. H. HUTTON, M.A.
 ESSAYS THEOLOGICAL AND LITERARY. New and cheaper issue. 2 vols. Globe 8vo. 6s. each.
 CONTENTS OF VOL. I.:—The moral significance of Atheism—The Atheistic Explanation of Religion—Science and Theism—Popular Pantheism—What is Revelation?—Christian Evidences, Popular and Critical—The Historical Problems of the Fourth Gospel—The Incarnation and Principles of Evidence—M. Renan's "Christ" —M. Renan's "St. Paul"—The Hard Church—Romanism, Protestantism, and Anglicanism.
 CONTENTS OF VOL. II.:—Goethe and his Influence—Wordsworth and his Genius —Shelley's Poetical Mysticism—Mr. Browning—The Poetry of the Old Testament —Arthur Hugh Clough—The Poetry of Matthew Arnold—Tennyson—Nathaniel Hawthorne.
 ESSAYS ON SOME OF THE MODERN GUIDES OF ENGLISH THOUGHT IN MATTERS OF FAITH. Globe 8vo. 6s.
 These essays deal with the following writers: Thomas Carlyle, Cardinal Newman, Matthew Arnold, George Eliot, and Frederick Denison Maurice.

INGRAM.—Works by T. DUNBAR INGRAM, LL.D.
 A HISTORY OF THE LEGISLATIVE UNION OF GREAT BRITAIN AND IRELAND. Demy 8vo. 10s. 6d.
 TWO CHAPTERS OF IRISH HISTORY. 8vo. [*Immediately.*

IONIA.—THE ANTIQUITIES OF IONIA, see under Dilettanti Society's Publications.

IRVING.—THE ANNALS OF OUR TIME. A Diurnal of Events, Social and Political, Home and Foreign, from the Accession of Queen Victoria to the Peace of Versailles. By JOSEPH IRVING. New Edition, revised. 8vo. half-bound. 18s.
 ANNALS OF OUR TIME. Supplements. From Feb. 28, 1871, to March 16, 1874. 8vo. 4s. 6d. From March, 1874, to the Occupation of Cyprus. 8vo. 4s. 6d. A Third Supplement is in the Press, bringing the work down to Jubilee day.

JAMES (Sir W. M.).—THE BRITISH IN INDIA. By the late Right Hon. Sir WILLIAM MILBOURNE JAMES, Lord Justice of Appeal. Edited by his Daughter, MARY J. SALIS SCHWABE. Demy 8vo. 12s. 6d.

JAMES.—Works by HENRY JAMES:
 FRENCH POETS AND NOVELISTS. New Edition. Crown 8vo. 4s. 6d.
 CONTENTS:—Alfred de Musset; Théophile Gautier; Baudelaire; Honoré de Balzac; George Sand; The Two Ampères; Turgénieff, &c.
 PORTRAITS OF PLACES. Crown 8vo. 7s. 6d.
 PARTIAL PORTRAITS. Crown 8vo. 6s.
 CONTENTS:—Emerson; The Life of George Eliot; Daniel Deronda; Anthony Trollope; R. L. Stevenson; Miss Woolson; Alphonse Daudet; Guy de Maupassant; Turgénieff; George du Maurier. These portrait studies are followed by an essay on *The Art of Fiction*.

JEBB.—MODERN GREECE. Two Lectures delivered before the Philosophical Institution of Edinburgh. With papers on "The Progress of Greece," and "Byron in Greece." By R. C. JEBB, M.A., LL.D. Edin. Professor of Greek in the University of Glasgow. Crown 8vo. 5s.

JENNINGS.—CHRONOLOGICAL TABLES: A Synchronistic Arrangement of the Events of Ancient History, with an Index. By the Rev. ARTHUR C. JENNINGS, Rector of King's Stanley, Gloucestershire. Author of "A Commentary on the Psalms," "Ecclesia Anglicana," "Manual of Church History,". &c. 8vo, 5s.

JEVONS.—LETTERS AND JOURNAL OF W. STANLEY JEVONS. Edited by his WIFE. With Portrait. Demy 8vo. 14s.

JOHNSON'S LIVES OF THE POETS.—The Six Chief Lives —Milton, Dryden, Swift, Addison, Pope, Gray. With Macaulay's "Life of Johnson." Edited, with Preface, by MATTHEW ARNOLD. New and Popular Edition. Crown 8vo. 4s. 6d.

HISTORY, BIOGRAPHY, TRAVELS, ETC.

KANT.—THE LIFE OF IMMANUEL KANT. By J. H. STUCKENBERG, D.D., late Professor in Wittenburg College, Ohio. With Portrait. 8vo. 14*s.*

KANT—MAX MÜLLER.—CRITIQUE OF PURE REASON BY IMMANUEL KANT. In commemoration of the Centenary of its first Publication. Translated into English by F. MAX MÜLLER. With an Historical Introduction by LUDWIG NOIRÉ. 2 vols. Demy 8vo. 16*s.* each.
Volume I. HISTORICAL INTRODUCTION, by LUDWIG NOIRÉ; &c. &c.
Volume II. CRITIQUE OF PURE REASON, translated by F. MAX MÜLLER.
For the convenience of Students these volumes are now sold separately.
Of Professor Max Müller's translation of *The Critique of Pure Reason*, the *Times* says:—"Through this translation Kant's work has for the first time become international—the common property of the whole world."

KEARY.—ANNIE KEARY: a Memoir. By ELIZA KEARY. With a Portrait. Third Thousand. New Edition. Crown 8vo. 4*s.* 6*d.*

KEATS.—LETTERS OF KEATS. Edited by SIDNEY COLVIN, Author of "Keats" (English Men of Letters Series). Globe 8vo. [*Immediately.*

KELLOGG.—THE LIGHT OF ASIA AND THE LIGHT OF THE WORLD. A Comparison of the Legend, the Doctrine, and the Ethics of the Buddha with the Story, the Doctrine, and the Ethics of Christ. By S. H. KELLOGG, D.D., Professor in the Western Theological Seminary, Alleghany, Pa., U.S.A., eleven years Missionary to India, Corresponding Member of the American Oriental Society, Author of "A Grammar of the Hindi Language and Dialects," &c. Crown 8vo. 7*s.* 6*d.*

KILLEN.—ECCLESIASTICAL HISTORY OF IRELAND, from the Earliest Date to the Present Time. By W. D. KILLEN, D.D., President of Assembly's College, Belfast, and Professor of Ecclesiastical History. Two Vols. 8vo. 25*s.*

KINGSLEY (CHARLES).—Works by the Rev. CHARLES KINGSLEY, M.A., late Rector of Eversley and Canon of Westminster. (For other Works by the same Author, *see* THEOLOGICAL and BELLES LETTRES CATALOGUES.)

AT LAST: A CHRISTMAS in the WEST INDIES. With nearly Fifty Illustrations. New Edition. Crown 8vo. 6*s.*

THE ROMAN AND THE TEUTON. A Series of Lectures delivered before the University of Cambridge. New and Cheaper Edition, with Preface by Professor MAX MÜLLER. Crown 8vo. 6*s.*

PLAYS AND PURITANS, and other Historical Essays. With Portrait of Sir WALTER RALEIGH. New Edition. Crown 8vo. 6*s.*
In addition to the Essay mentioned in the title, this volume contains other two—one on "Sir Walter Raleigh and his Time," and one on Froude's "History of England."

HISTORICAL LECTURES AND ESSAYS. Crown 8vo. 6*s.*
SANITARY AND SOCIAL LECTURES AND ESSAYS. Crown 8vo. 6*s.*
SCIENTIFIC LECTURES AND ESSAYS. Crown 8vo. 6*s.*
LITERARY AND GENERAL LECTURES. Crown 8vo. 6*s.*
GLAUCUS: OR THE WONDERS OF THE SHORE. With Coloured Illustrations. Crown 8vo. 6*s.* Also a Presentation Edition in Ornamental Binding, gilt edges. Crown 8vo. 7*s.* 6*d.*

KINGSLEY (HENRY).—TALES OF OLD TRAVEL. Re-narrated by HENRY KINGSLEY, F.R.G.S. With Eight Illustrations by HUARD. Sixth Edition. Crown 8vo. 5*s.*

LABBERTON.—AN HISTORICAL ATLAS. Comprising 141 Maps, to which is added, besides an Explanatory Text on the period delineated in each Map, a carefully selected Bibliography of the English Books and Magazine Articles bearing on that period. By ROBERT H LABBERTON, Litt. Hum. Doctor. New Edition, Revised and Enlarged. 4to. 15*s.*

LAMB.—Works by CHARLES LAMB. Edited with Introduction and Notes by ALFRED AINGER, M.A., Canon of Bristol.
TALES FROM SHAKESPEARE. Globe 8vo. 5*s.* Golden Treasury Edition. 18mo. 4*s.* 6*d.* Globe Readings Edition for Schools. Globe 8vo. 2*s.*
ESSAYS OF ELIA. Globe 8vo. 5*s.*
POEMS, PLAYS, AND MISCELLANEOUS ESSAYS, &c. Globe 8vo. 5*s.*
MRS. LEICESTER'S SCHOOL; The Adventures of Ulysses; and other Essays. Globe 8vo. 5*s.*
LETTERS OF CHARLES LAMB. 2 vols. Globe 8vo. 10*s.*
CHARLES LAMB. By ALFRED AINGER. Uniform with Mr. Ainger's Edition of The Works of Charles Lamb." Globe 8vo. 5*s.*

LANFREY.—HISTORY OF NAPOLEON I. By P. LANFREY. A Translation made with the sanction of the author. New and Popular Edition. 4 vols. Crown 8vo. 30s.

LECTURES ON ART.—Delivered in support of the Society for Protection of Ancient Buildings. By REGD. STUART POOLE, Professor W. B. RICHMOND, E. J. POYNTER, R.A., J. T. MICKLETHWAITE, and WILLIAM MORRIS. Crown 8vo. 4s. 6d.

LETHBRIDGE.—A SHORT MANUAL OF THE HISTORY OF INDIA, with an account of INDIA AS IT IS. The Soil, Climate, and Productions; the People—their Races, Religions, Public Works, and Industries; the Civil Services and System of Administration. By Sir ROPER LETHBRIDGE, M.A., C.I.E., Press Commissioner with the Government of India, late Scholar of Exeter College. &c. &c. With Maps. Crown 8vo. 5s.

LIECHTENSTEIN.—HOLLAND HOUSE. By Princess MARIE LIECHTENSTEIN. With Five Steel Engravings by C. H. JEENS, after paintings by WATTS and other celebrated Artists, and numerous Illustrations drawn by Professor P. H. DELAMOTTE, and engraved on Wood by J. D. COOPER, W. PALMER. and JEWITT & Co., about 40 Illustrations by the Woodbury-type process, and India Proofs of the Steel Engravings. Two vols. Medium 4to., half morocco elegant. 4l. 4s.

LUBBOCK.—Works by Sir JOHN LUBBOCK, Bart., M.P., D.C.L., F.R.S.
ADDRESSES, POLITICAL AND EDUCATIONAL. 8vo. 8s. 6d.
FIFTY YEARS OF SCIENCE. Being the address delivered at York to the British Association. August, 1881. 8vo. 2s. 6d.
THE PLEASURES OF LIFE. Twelfth and Cheaper Edition. Fcap. 8vo. 1s. 6d. cloth; 1s. sewed.

LYTE.—Works by H. C. MAXWELL-LYTE, F.S.A., Deputy Deeper of the Public Records.
ETON COLLEGE, HISTORY OF, 1440—1875. With Illustrations. New and cheaper issue. 8vo. 21s.
A HISTORY OF THE UNIVERSITY OF OXFORD. From the Earliest Times to the Year 1530. 8vo. 16s.

MACARTHUR.—HISTORY OF SCOTLAND. By MARGARET MACARTHUR. Being the Third Volume of the Historical Course for Schools, Edited by EDWARD A. FREEMAN, D.C.L. New Edition. 18mo. 2s.

McLENNAN.—Works by JOHN FERGUSON McLENNAN.
THE PATRIARCHAL THEORY. Based on Papers of the late JOHN FERGUSON McLENNAN. Edited and completed by DONALD McLENNAN, of the Inner Temple, Barrister-at-Law. 8vo. 14s.
STUDIES IN ANCIENT HISTORY. Comprising a Reprint of "Primitive Marriage: an Inquiry into the Origin of the Form of Capture in Marriage Ceremonies." A New Edition. 8vo. 16s.

MACMILLAN (REV. HUGH).—For other Works by same Author, see THEOLOGICAL and SCIENTIFIC CATALOGUES.
HOLIDAYS ON HIGH LANDS; or, Rambles and Incidents in search of Alpine Plants. Second Edition, revised and enlarged. Globe 8vo. 6s.
ROMAN MOSAICS; or Studies in Rome and its Neighbourhood. Globe 8vo. 6s.

MACMILLAN (DANIEL).—MEMOIR OF DANIEL MACMILLAN. By THOMAS HUGHES, Q.C., Author of "Tom Brown's Schooldays," etc. With Portrait engraved on Steel by C. H. JEENS, from a Painting by LOWES DICKINSON. Fifth Thousand. Crown 8vo. 4s. 6d.—POPULAR EDITION, Paper Covers 1s.

MACREADY.—MACREADY'S REMINISCENCES AND SELECTIONS FROM HIS DIARIES AND LETTERS. Edited by Sir F POLLOCK, Bart., one of his Executors. With Four Portraits engraved by JEENS. New and Cheaper Edition. Crown 8vo. 7s. 6d.

MAHAFFY.—Works by the Rev. J. P. MAHAFFY, M.A., Fellow of Trinity College, Dublin:—
SOCIAL LIFE IN GREECE FROM HOMER TO MENANDER. Fifth Edition, revised and enlarged, with a new chapter on Greek Art. Crown 8vo.
GREEK LIFE AND THOUGHT FROM THE AGE OF ALEXANDER TO THE ROMAN CONQUEST. Crown 8vo. 12s. 6d.
RAMBLES AND STUDIES IN GREECE. With Map and Illustrations. Third Edition. Crown 8vo. 10s. 6d.
SKETCHES FROM A TOUR THROUGH HOLLAND AND GERMANY. By J. P. MAHAFFY and J. E. ROGERS. With Illustrations by J. E. ROGERS. Extra Crown 8vo. [*Immediately.*

MARGARY.—THE JOURNEY OF AUGUSTUS RAYMOND MARGARY FROM SHANGHAE TO BHAMO AND BACK TO MANWYNE. From his Journals and Letters, with a brief Biographical Preface, a concluding chapter by Sir RUTHERFORD ALCOCK, K.C.B., and a Steel Portrait engraved by JEENS, and Map. 8vo. 10s. 6d.

MARTEL.—MILITARY ITALY. By CHARLES MARTEL. With Map. 8vo. 12s. 6d.

MARTIN.—THE HISTORY OF LLOYD'S, AND OF MARINE INSURANCE IN GREAT BRITAIN. With an Appendix containing Statistics relating to Marine Insurance. By FREDERICK MARTIN. 8vo. 14s.

MARTINEAU.—BIOGRAPHICAL SKETCHES, 1852-75. By HARRIET MARTINEAU. With Four Additional Sketches, and Autobiographical Sketch. Fifth Edition. Crown 8vo. 6s. (Biographical Series.)

MASSON (DAVID).—By DAVID MASSON, LL.D., Professor of Rhetoric and English Literature in the University of Edinburgh. For other Works by same Author, see PHILOSOPHICAL and BELLES LETTRES CATALOGUE.
CHATTERTON: A Story of the Year 1770. Crown 8vo. 5s.
THE THREE DEVILS: Luther's, Goethe's, and Milton's; and other Essays. Crown 8vo. 5s.
WORDSWORTH, SHELLEY, AND KEATS; and other Essays. Crown 8vo. 5s.
CARLYLE PERSONALLY AND IN HIS WRITINGS. Two Lectures. Extra fcap. 8vo. 2s. 6d.

MATHEWS.—LIFE OF CHARLES J. MATHEWS, Chiefly Autobiographical. With Selections from his Correspondence and Speeches. Edited by CHARLES DICKENS. Two Vols. 8vo. 25s.

MAURICE.—LIFE OF FREDERICK DENISON MAURICE. Chiefly told in his own Letters. Edited by his Son, FREDERICK MAURICE. With Two Portraits. Third Edition. 2 vols. Demy 8vo. 36s.
Popular Edition. 2 vols. Crown 8vo. 16s.

MAURICE.—THE FRIENDSHIP OF BOOKS; AND OTHER LECTURES. By the Rev. F. D. MAURICE. Edited with Preface, by THOMAS HUGHES, Q.C. Crown 8vo. 4s. 6d.

MAURICE.—LETTERS FROM DONEGAL IN 1826. By a LADY "FELON." Edited by Colonel MAURICE, Professor of Military History, Royal Staff College. Crown 8vo. 1s.

MAXWELL.—PROFESSOR CLERK MAXWELL, A LIFE OF. With a Selection from his Correspondence and Occasional Writings, and a Sketch of his Contributions to Science. By LEWIS CAMPBELL, M.A., LL.D., Professor of Greek in the University of St. Andrews, and Professor WILLIAM GARNETT, M.A., Principal of Durham College of Science, Newcastle-upon-Tyne. New Edition, Abridged and Revised. Crown 8vo. 7s. 6d.

MAYOR (J. E. B.)—Works edited by JOHN E. B. MAYOR, M.A., Kennedy Professor of Latin at Cambridge:—
CAMBRIDGE IN THE SEVENTEENTH CENTURY. Part II. Autobiography of Matthew Robinson. Fcap. 8vo. 5s. 6d.

MELBOURNE.—MEMOIRS OF THE RT. HON. WILLIAM, SECOND VISCOUNT MELBOURNE. By W. M. TORRENS, M.P. With Portrait after Sir T. Lawrence. Second Edition. Two Vols. 8vo. 32s.

MELDOLA.—REPORT ON THE EAST ANGLIAN EARTHQUAKE OF APRIL 22ND, 1884. Being Vol. L of the Essex Field Club Special Memoirs, by RAPHAEL MELDOLA, F.C.S., F.I.C., F.R.A.S., etc., Professor of Chemistry in the Finsbury Technical College, City Guilds of London Institute, and WILLIAM WHITE, F.S.E., Members of the Geologists' Association. (Drawn up by R. MELDOLA, and read in abstract at the meeting of the Essex Field Club, February 28th, 1885.) With Maps and other Illustrations. Cheaper issue. Demy 8vo. 3s. 6d.

MERCIER.—THE NERVOUS SYSTEM AND THE MIND: a Treatise on the Dynamics of the Human Organism. By CHARLES MERCIER, M.B. Demy 8vo. 12s. 6d.

MIALL.—LIFE OF EDWARD MIALL, formerly M.P. for Rochdale and Bradford. By his Son, ARTHUR MIALL. With a Portrait. 8vo. 10s. 6d.

MICHELET.—A SUMMARY OF MODERN HISTORY. Translated from the French of M. MICHELET, and continued to the present time by M. C. M. SIMPSON. Globe 8vo. 4s. 6d.

MILLET.—JEAN FRANÇOIS MILLET; Peasant and Painter. Translated from the French of ALFRED SENSIER. With numerous Illustrations. Globe 4to. 16s.

MILTON.—LIFE OF JOHN MILTON. Narrated in connection with the Political, Ecclesiastical, and Literary History of his Time. By DAVID MASSON, M.A., LL.D., Professor of Rhetoric and English Literature in the University of Edinburgh. With Portraits. Vol. I. 1608—1639. New and Revised Edition. 8vo. 21s. Vol. II. 1638—1643. 8vo. 16s. Vol. III. 1643—1649. 8vo. 18s. Vols. IV. and V. 1649—1660. 32s. Vol. VI. 1660—1674. With Portrait. 21s. [*Index Volume in preparation.*
This work is not only a Biography, but also a continuous Political, Ecclesiastical, and Literary History of England through Milton's whole time.

MITFORD (A. B.)—TALES OF OLD JAPAN. By A. B. MITFORD. Second Secretary to the British Legation in Japan. With upwards of 30 Illustrations, drawn and cut on Wood by Japanese Artists. New and Cheaper Edition. Crown 8vo. 6s.

MORLEY.—Works by JOHN MORLEY. New Collected Edition. In 10 vols. Globe 8vo. 5s. each.
VOLTAIRE. 1 vol.
ROUSSEAU. 2 vols.
DIDEROT AND THE ENCYCLOPÆDISTS. 2 vols.
ON COMPROMISE. 1 vol.
MISCELLANIES. 3 vols.
BURKE. 1 vol.
BURKE. (*English Men of Letters Series.*) Crown 8vo. Library Edition, 2s.6d. Popular Edition, sewed, 1s.; cloth, 1s. 6d.
ON THE STUDY OF LITERATURE. The Annual Address to the Students of the London Society for the extension of University Teaching. Delivered at the Mansion House, February 26th, 1887. Crown 8vo. 1s. 6d.

MOSS.—A SEASON IN SUTHERLAND. By JOHN E. EDWARDS-MOSS. Crown 8vo. 4s. 6d.

MURRAY.—ROUND ABOUT FRANCE. By E. C. GRENVILLE MURRAY. Crown 8vo. 7s. 6d.

MUSIC.—DICTIONARY OF MUSIC AND MUSICIANS (A.D. 1450—1888). By Eminent Writers, English and Foreign. Edited by SIR GEORGE GROVE, D.C.L., Director of the Royal College of Music. Three Vols. 8vo. With Illustrations and Woodcuts. Parts I. to XIV., XIX. to XXII. 3s. 6d. each. Parts XV. and XVI., 7s. Parts XVII. and XVIII., 7s. Vols. I., II., and III. 8vo. 21s. each.
Vol. I.—A to Impromptu. Vol. II.—Improperia to Plain Song. Vol. III. Planché to Sumer is Icumen in.
*** Part XXII. completes the "Dictionary of Music and Musicians" as originally contemplated. But an Appendix and a Full General Index are in the Press.

MYERS.—ESSAYS BY FREDERIC W. H. MYERS. 2 vols. 1. Classical. II. Modern. Crown 8vo. 4s. 6d. each.

NAPOLEON.—THE HISTORY OF NAPOLEON I. By P. LANFREY. A Translation with the sanction of the Author. New and Popular Edition. Four Vols. Crown 8vo. 30s.

NEWTON.—ESSAYS ON ART AND ARCHÆOLOGY. By Sir CHARLES THOMAS NEWTON, C.B., Ph.D., D.C.L., LL.D., late Keeper of Greek and Roman Antiquities at the British Museum, &c. 8vo. 12s. 6d.

NORDENSKIÖLD'S ARCTIC VOYAGES, 1858-79.—With Maps and numerous Illustrations. 8vo. 16s.
VOYAGE OF THE *VEGA*. By ADOLF ERIK NORDENSKIÖLD. Translated by ALEXANDER LESLIE. With numerous Illustrations, Maps, &c. Popular and Cheaper Edition. Crown 8vo. 6s.

NORGATE.—ENGLAND UNDER THE ANGEVIN KINGS. By KATE NORGATE. With Maps and Plans. 2 vols. 8vo. 32s.

HISTORY, BIOGRAPHY, TRAVELS, ETC.

OLIPHANT (MRS.).—Works by Mrs. OLIPHANT.
THE MAKERS OF FLORENCE: Dante, Giotto, Savonarola, and their City. With numerous Illustrations from drawings by Professor DELAMOTTE, and portrait of Savonarola, engraved by JEENS. New and Cheaper Edition. Crown 8vo. 10s. 6d.
THE MAKERS OF VENICE. Doges, Conquerors, Painters, and Men of Letters. With numerous Illustrations. New and Cheaper Edition. Crown 8vo. 10s. 6d.
THE LITERARY HISTORY OF ENGLAND IN THE END OF THE EIGHTEENTH AND BEGINNING OF THE NINETEENTH CENTURY. New Issue, with a Preface. 3 vols. Demy 8vo. 21s.

OLIPHANT.—THE DUKE AND THE SCHOLAR; and other Essays. By T. L. KINGTON OLIPHANT. 8vo. 7s. 6d.

OLIVER.—MADAGASCAR: an Historical and Descriptive Account of the Island and its former Dependencies. Compiled by Captain S. PASFIELD OLIVER, F.S.A., F.R.G.S., late Royal Artillery. With Maps. 2 vols. Medium 8vo. £2 12s. 6d.

OTTE.—SCANDINAVIAN HISTORY. By E. C. OTTE. With Maps. Extra fcap. 8vo. 6s.

OWENS COLLEGE ESSAYS AND ADDRESSES.—By PROFESSORS' AND LECTURERS OF OWENS COLLEGE, MANCHESTER. Published in Commemoration of the Opening of the New College Buildings, October 7th, 1873. 8vo. 14s.

PALGRAVE (R. F. D.)—THE HOUSE OF COMMONS; Illustrations of its History and Practice. By REGINALD F. D. PALGRAVE, Clerk Assistant of the House of Commons. New and Revised Edition. Crown 8vo. 2s. 6d.

PALGRAVE (SIR F.)—HISTORY OF NORMANDY AND OF ENGLAND. By Sir FRANCIS PALGRAVE, Deputy Keeper of Her Majesty's Public Records. Completing the History to the Death of William Rufus. 4 Vols. 8vo. 4l. 4s

PALGRAVE (W. G.)—Works by WILLIAM GIFFORD PALGRAVE, late H.M. Minister Resident in Uruguay.
A NARRATIVE OF A YEAR'S JOURNEY THROUGH CENTRAL AND EASTERN ARABIA, 1862–3. Seventh Edition. With Maps, Plans, and Portrait of Author, engraved on steel by JEENS. Crown 8vo. 6s.
ESSAYS ON EASTERN QUESTIONS. 8vo. 10s. 6d.
DUTCH GUIANA. With Maps and Plans. 8vo. 9s.
ULYSSES; OR, SCENES AND STUDIES IN MANY LANDS. 8vo. 12s. 6d.

PARKMAN.—Works by FRANCIS PARKMAN.
MONTCALM AND WOLFE. Library Edition. Illustrated with Portraits and Maps. 2 vols. 8vo. 12s. 6d. each.
THE COLLECTED WORKS OF FRANCIS PARKMAN. Popular Edition. In 10 vols. Crown 8vo. 7s. 6d. each, or complete £3 13s. 6d.
PIONEERS OF FRANCE IN THE NEW WORLD. 1 vol.
THE JESUITS IN NORTH AMERICA. 1 vol.
LA SALLE AND THE DISCOVERY OF THE GREAT WEST. 1 vol.
THE OREGON TRAIL. 1 vol.
THE OLD RÉGIME IN CANADA UNDER LOUIS XIV. 1 vol.
COUNT FRONTENAC AND NEW FRANCE UNDER LOUIS XIV. 1 vol.
MONTCALM AND WOLFE. 2 vols.
THE CONSPIRACY OF PONTIAC. 2 vols.

PATER.—THE RENAISSANCE: Studies in Art and Poetry. By WALTER PATER, Fellow of Brasenose College, Author of "Marius the Epicurean: his Sensations and Ideas," "Imaginary Portraits." Fourth Thousand, Revised and Enlarged. Extra Crown 8vo. 10s. 6d.

PATTESON.—LIFE AND LETTERS OF JOHN COLERIDGE PATTESON, D.D., Missionary Bishop of the Melanesian Islands. By CHARLOTTE M. YONGE, Author of "The Heir of Redclyffe." With Portraits after RICHMOND and from Photograph, engraved by JEENS. With Map. New Edition. Two Vols. Crown 8vo. 12s.

PATTISON.—MEMOIRS. By MARK PATTISON, late Rector of Lincoln College, Oxford. Crown 8vo. 8s. 6d.

PAYNE.—A HISTORY OF EUROPEAN COLONIES. By E. J. PAYNE, M.A. With Maps. 18mo. 4s. 6d. [*Historical Course for Schools.*

STRANGFORD.—EGYPTIAN SHRINES AND SYRIAN SEPULCHRES, including a Visit to Palmyra. By EMILY A. BEAUFORT (Viscountess Strangford), Author of "The Eastern Shores of the Adriatic." New Edition. Crown 8vo. 7s. 6d.

TAIT.—AN ANALYSIS OF ENGLISH HISTORY, based upon Green's "Short History of the English People." By C. W. A. TAIT, M.A., Assistant Master, Clifton College. Crown 8vo. 3s. 6d.

TAIT.—CATHARINE AND CRAUFURD TAIT, WIFE AND SON OF ARCHIBALD CAMPBELL, ARCHBISHOP OF CANTERBURY: a Memoir, Edited, at the request of the Archbishop, by the Rev. W. BENHAM, B.D., Rector of St. Edmund-the-King and St. Nicholas Acons, One of the Six Preachers of Canterbury Cathedral. With Two Portraits engraved by JEENS. New and Cheaper Edition. Crown 8vo. 6s. (Biographical Series.) Abridged Edition. Crown 8vo. 2s. 6d.

TAIT.—THE LIFE OF ARCHIBALD CAMPBELL TAIT, Archbishop of Canterbury. By the Very Rev. the DEAN OF WINDSOR and Rev. W. BENHAM, B.D. 2 vols. 8vo. [*In the press.*

TERESA.—THE LIFE OF ST. TERESA. By MARIA TRENCH. With Portrait engraved by JEENS. Crown 8vo, cloth extra. 8s. 6d.

THOMPSON.—HISTORY OF ENGLAND. By EDITH THOMPSON Being Vol. II. of the Historical Course for Schools, Edited by EDWARD A FREEMAN, D.C.L. New Edition, revised and enlarged, with Coloured Maps 18mo. 2s. 6d.

THOMPSON.—PUBLIC OPINION AND LORD BEACONSFIELD, 1875-1880. By GEO. CARSLAKE THOMPSON, LL.M., of the Inner Temple, Barrister-at-Law. 2 vols. Demy 8vo. 36s.

THROUGH THE RANKS TO A COMMISSION.—New and Popular Edition. Crown 8vo. 2s. 6d.

TODHUNTER.—THE CONFLICT OF STUDIES; AND OTHER ESSAYS ON SUBJECTS CONNECTED WITH EDUCATION. By ISAAC TODHUNTER, M.A., F.R.S., late Fellow and Principal Mathematical Lecturer of St. John's College, Cambridge. 8vo. 10s. 6d.

TROLLOPE.—A HISTORY OF THE COMMONWEALTH OF FLORENCE FROM THE EARLIEST INDEPENDENCE OF THE COMMUNE TO THE FALL OF THE REPUBLIC IN 1831. By T. ADOLPHUS TROLLOPE. 4 Vols. 8vo. Cloth, 21s.

TURNER.—SAMOA. A Hundred Years ago and long before, together with Notes on the Cults and Customs of Twenty-three other Islands in the Pacific. By GEORGE TURNER, LL.D., of the London Missionary Society. With a Preface by E. B. TYLOR, F.R.S. With Maps. Crown 8vo. 9s.

TYLOR.—ANTHROPOLOGY: an Introduction to the Study of Man and Civilisation. By E. B. TYLOR, D.C.L., F.R.S. With Illustrations. Crown 8vo. 7s. 6d.

UNKNOWN COUNTRY, AN.—(THE RECORD OF A JOURNEY IN IRELAND.) By the Author of "John Halifax, Gentleman." With Illustrations by F. NOEL PATON. Royal 8vo. 7s. 6d.

UPPINGHAM BY THE SEA.—A NARRATIVE OF THE YEAR AT BORTH. By J. H. S. Crown 8vo. 3s. 6d.

VERNEY.—HOW THE PEASANT OWNER LIVES IN PARTS OF FRANCE, GERMANY, ITALY, AND RUSSIA. By LADY VERNEY. Crown 8vo. 3s. 6d.

VICTOR EMMANUEL II., FIRST KING OF ITALY. By G. S. GODKIN. New Edition. Crown 8vo. 6s. (Biographical Series.)

WALLACE.—THE MALAY ARCHIPELAGO: the Land of the Orang Utan and the Bird of Paradise. By ALFRED RUSSEL WALLACE. A Narrative of Travel with Studies of Man and Nature. With Maps and numerous Illustrations. Eighth Edition. Crown 8vo. 7s. 6d.

WALLACE (D. M.)—EGYPT: and the Egyptian Question. By D. MACKENZIE WALLACE, M.A., Author of "Russia: a Six Years' Residence," &c. 8vo. 14s.

WARD.—WILLIAM GEORGE WARD AND THE OXFORD MOVEMENT. By WILFRID WARD. With Portrait. 1 vol. 8vo. [*Immediately*

HISTORY, BIOGRAPHY, TRAVELS ETC.

WARD.—A HISTORY OF ENGLISH DRAMATIC LITERATURE TO THE DEATH OF QUEEN ANNE. By A. W. WARD, M.A., Professor of History and English Literature in Owens College, Manchester. Two Vols. 8vo. 32s.

WARD (J.)—EXPERIENCES OF A DIPLOMATIST. Being recollections of Germany founded on Diaries kept during the years 1840—1870. By JOHN WARD, C.B., late H.M. Minister-Resident to the Hanse Towns. 8vo. 10s. 6d.

WARD.—ENGLISH POETS. Selections, with Critical Introductions by various writers, and a General Introduction by MATTHEW ARNOLD. Edited by T. H. WARD, M.A. 4 vols. New Edition. Crown 8vo. 7s. 6d. each.
Vol. I. CHAUCER to DONNE.
Vol. II. BEN JONSON to DRYDEN.
Vol. III. ADDISON to BLAKE.
Vol. IV. WORDSWORTH to ROSSETTI.

WATERTON (C.)—WANDERINGS IN SOUTH AMERICA, THE NORTH-WEST OF THE UNITED STATES, AND THE ANTILLES IN 1812, 1816, 1820, and 1824. With Original Instructions for the perfect Preservation of Birds, etc., for Cabinets of Natural History. By CHARLES WATERTON. New Edition, edited with Biographical Introduction and Explanatory Index by the Rev. J. G. WOOD. M.A. With 100 Illustrations. Cheaper Edition. Crown 8vo. 6s.
PEOPLE'S ILLUSTRATED EDITION. Demy 4to. 6d.

WATSON.—A VISIT TO WAZAN, THE SACRED CITY OF MOROCCO By ROBERT SPENCE WATSON. With Illustrations. 8vo. 10s. 6d.

WATSON (ELLEN.)—A RECORD OF ELLEN WATSON. Arranged and Edited by ANNA BUCKLAND. With Portrait. Third Edition. Crown 8vo. 6s. (Biographical Series.)

WESLEY.—JOHN WESLEY AND THE EVANGELICAL REACTION of the Eighteenth Century. By JULIA WEDGWOOD. Crown 8vo. 8s. 6d.

WHEELER.—Works by J. TALBOYS WHEELER, late Assistant-Secretary to the Government of India, Foreign Department, and late Secretary to the Government of British Burma.
A SHORT HISTORY OF INDIA, AND OF THE FRONTIER STATES OF AFGHANISTAN, NEPAUL, AND BURMA. With Maps and Tables. Crown 8vo. 12s.
COLLEGE HISTORY OF INDIA, ASIATIC AND EUROPEAN. Crown 8vo. 3s. 6d.
INDIA UNDER BRITISH RULE FROM THE FOUNDATION OF THE EAST INDIA COMPANY. Demy 8vo. 12s. 6d.

WHEWELL.—WILLIAM WHEWELL, D.D., late Master of Trinity College, Cambridge. An account of his Writings, with Selections from his Literary and Scientific correspondence. By I. TODHUNTER, M.A., F.R.S. Two Vols. 8vo. 25s.

WHITE.—THE NATURAL HISTORY AND ANTIQUITIES OF SELBORNE. By GILBERT WHITE. Edited, with Memoir and Notes, by FRANK BUCKLAND, A Chapter on Antiquities by LORD SELBORNE, and numerous Illustrations by P. H. DELAMOTTE. New and Cheaper Edition. Crown 8vo. 6s.
Also a Large Paper Edition, containing, in addition to the above, upwards of Thirty Woodburytype Illustrations from Drawings by Prof. DELAMOTTE. Two Vols. 4to. Half morocco, elegant. 4l. 4s.

WILSON.—A MEMOIR OF GEORGE WILSON, M.D., F.R.S.E., Regius Professor of Technology in the University of Edinburgh. By his SISTER. New Edition. Crown 8vo. 6s.

WILSON (DANIEL, LL.D.)—Works by DANIEL WILSON, LL.D Professor of History and English Literature in University College, Toronto:—
PREHISTORIC ANNALS OF SCOTLAND. New Edition, with numerous Illustrations. Two Vols. Demy 8vo. 36s.
PREHISTORIC MAN : Researches into the Origin of Civilisation in the Old and New World. New Edition, revised and enlarged throughout, with numerous Illustrations and Two Coloured Plates. Two Vols. 8vo. 36s.
CHATTERTON : A Biographical Study. Crown 8vo. 6s. 6d.

FISKE.—AMERICAN POLITICAL IDEAS VIEWED FROM THE STANDPOINT OF UNIVERSAL HISTORY. Three Lectures delivered at the Royal Institution of Great Britain. By JOHN FISKE, Author of "Darwinism: and other Essays," "Excursions of an Evolutionist," &c. Crown 8vo. 4s.

GOSCHEN.—REPORTS AND SPEECHES ON LOCAL TAXATION. By The Right Hon. GEORGE J. GOSCHEN. M.P. Royal 8vo. 5s.

GUIDE TO THE UNPROTECTED, in Every Day Matters Relating to Property and Income. By a BANKER'S DAUGHTER. Fifth Edition, Revised. Extra fcap. 8vo. 3s. 6d.

GUNTON.—WEALTH AND PROGRESS. A Critical Examination of the Wages Question and its Economic Relation to Social Reform. By GEORGE GUNTON. Crown 8vo. 6s.

HARWOOD.—Works by GEORGE HARWOOD, M.A.
DISESTABLISHMENT: a Defence of the Principle of a National Church. 8vo. 12s.
THE COMING DEMOCRACY. Crown 8vo. 6s.

HILL.—Works by OCTAVIA HILL :—
OUR COMMON LAND; and other Short Essays. Extra fcap. 8vo. 3s. 6d.
CONTENTS :—Our Common Land. District Visiting. A more Excellent Way of Charity. A Word on Good Citizenship. Open Spaces. Effectual Charity. The Future of our Commons.
HOMES OF THE LONDON POOR. Popular Edition. Cr. 8vo. Sewed. 1s.

HOLLAND.—THE TREATY RELATIONS OF RUSSIA AND TURKEY FROM 1774 TO 1853. A Lecture delivered at Oxford, April 1877. By T. E. HOLLAND, D.C.L., Professor of International Law and Diplomacy, Oxford. Crown 8vo. 2s.

HOLMES.—THE COMMON LAW. By O. W. HOLMES, jun. Demy 8vo. 12s.

HORTON.—THE SILVER POUND AND ENGLAND'S MONETARY POLICY since the Restoration, together with a History of the Guinea, illustrated by contemporary documents. By the HON. S. DANA HORTON, a Delegate of the United States to the International Monetary Conferences of 1878 and 1881. 8vo. 14s.

JEVONS.—Works by W. STANLEY JEVONS, LL.D., M.A., F.R.S. (For other Works by the same Author, see EDUCATIONAL and PHILOSOPHICAL CATALOGUES.)
THE THEORY OF POLITICAL ECONOMY. Second Edition, revised, with new Preface and Appendices. 8vo. 10s. 6d.
PRIMER OF POLITICAL ECONOMY. 18mo. 1s.
METHODS OF SOCIAL REFORM, and other Papers. Demy 8vo. 10s. 6d.
INVESTIGATIONS IN CURRENCY AND FINANCE. Edited, with an Introduction, by H. S. FOXWELL, M.A., Fellow and Lecturer of St. John's College, Cambridge, and Professor of Political Economy at University College, London. Illustrated by 20 Diagrams. Demy 8vo. 21s.

LIGHTWOOD.—THE NATURE OF POSITIVE LAW. By JOHN M. LIGHTWOOD, M.A., of Lincoln's Inn, Barrister-at-Law, Fellow of Trinity Hall Cambridge. Demy 8vo. 12s. 6d.

LOWELL.—Works by JAMES RUSSELL LOWELL..
DEMOCRACY; and other Addresses. Crown 8vo. 5s.
POLITICAL ESSAYS. Extra Crown 8vo. 7s. 6d.

LUBBOCK.—ADDRESSES, POLITICAL AND EDUCATIONAL. By Sir JOHN LUBBOCK, Bart., M.P., &c., &c. 8vo. 8s. 6d.

MACDONELL.—THE LAND QUESTION, WITH SPECIAL REFERENCE TO ENGLAND AND SCOTLAND. By JOHN MACDONELL Barrister-at-Law. 8vo. 10s. 6d.

MAITLAND.—PLEAS OF THE CROWN FOR THE COUNTY OF GLOUCESTER, BEFORE THE ABBOT OF READING AND HIS FELLOW JUSTICES ITINERANT, IN THE FIFTH YEAR OF THE REIGN OF KING HENRY THE THIRD AND THE YEAR OF GRACE, 1221. Edited by F. W. MAITLAND. 8vo. 7s. 6d.

MARSHALL.—THE ECONOMICS OF INDUSTRY. By A. MARSHALL, M.A., Professor of Political Economy in the University of Cambridge, late Principal of University College Bristol, and MARY PALEY MARSHALL, late Lecturer at Newnham Hall, Cambridge. Extra fcap. 8vo. 2s. 6d.

MONAHAN.—THE METHOD OF LAW: an Essay on the Statement and Arrangement of the Legal Standard of Conduct. By J. H. MONAHAN, Q.C. Crown 8vo. 6s.

PATERSON.—Works by JAMES PATERSON, M.A., Barrister-at-Law, sometime Commissioner for English and Irish Fisheries, &c.
THE LIBERTY OF THE SUBJECT AND THE LAWS OF ENGLAND RELATING TO THE SECURITY OF THE PERSON. Commentaries on. Cheaper issue. Crown 8vo. 21s.
THE LIBERTY OF THE PRESS, OF SPEECH, AND OF PUBLIC WORSHIP. Being Commentaries on the Liberty of the Subject and the Laws of England. Crown 8vo. 12s.

PHILLIMORE.—PRIVATE LAW AMONG THE ROMANS, from the Pandects. By JOHN GEORGE PHILLIMORE, Q.C. 8vo. 16s.

POLLOCK (F.).—ESSAYS IN JURISPRUDENCE AND ETHICS. By FREDERICK POLLOCK, M.A., LL.D., Corpus Christi Professor of Jurisprudence in the University of Oxford; late Fellow of Trinity College, Camb. 8vo. 10s. 6d.

PRACTICAL POLITICS.—ISSUED BY THE NATIONAL LIBERAL FEDERATION. Complete in one volume. 8vo. 6s. Or:—
I. THE TENANT FARMER: Land Laws and Landlords. By JAMES HOWARD. 8vo. 1s.
II. FOREIGN POLICY. By Right Hon. M. E. GRANT DUFF, M.P. 8vo. 1s.
III. FREEDOM OF LAND. By G. SHAW LEFEVRE, M.P. 8vo. 2s. 6d.
IV. BRITISH COLONIAL POLICY. By Sir DAVID WEDDERBURN, Bart., M.P. 8vo. 1s.

PRICE.—INDUSTRIAL PEACE: Its Advantages, Methods, and Difficulties. A Report of an Inquiry made for the Toynbee Trustees. By L. L. F. R. PRICE, formerly Scholar of Trinity College, Oxford. With a Preface by ALFRED MARSHALL, Professor of Political Economy in the University of Cambridge. With Portrait of Arnold Toynbee. Medium 8vo. 6s.

RICHEY.—THE IRISH LAND LAWS. By ALEXANDER G. RICHEY, Q.C., LL.D., Deputy Regius Professor of Feudal and English Law in the University of Dublin. Crown 8vo. 3s. 6d.

SIDGWICK.—Works by HENRY SIDGWICK, M.A., LL.D., Knightbridge Professor of Moral Philosophy in the University of Cambridge, &c.:
THE PRINCIPLES OF POLITICAL ECONOMY. Second Edition, Revised. Demy 8vo. 16s.
THE METHODS OF ETHICS. Third Edition, Revised and Enlarged. Demy 8vo. 14s.
A SUPPLEMENT TO THE SECOND EDITION. Containing all the Important Additions and Alterations in the Third Edition. Demy 8vo. 6s.
THE SCOPE AND METHOD OF ECONOMIC SCIENCE. An Address delivered to the Economic Science and Statistics Section of the British Association at Aberdeen, 1885. Crown 8vo. 2s.
OUTLINES OF THE HISTORY OF ETHICS FOR ENGLISH READERS. Second Edition, Revised. Crown 8vo. 3s. 6d.

STATESMAN'S YEAR BOOK, THE: A STATISTICAL AND HISTORICAL ANNUAL OF THE STATES OF THE CIVILIZED WORLD, FOR THE YEAR 1888. Twenty-fifth Annual Publication. Revised after Official Returns. Edited by J. SCOTT KELTIE. Crown 8vo. 10s. 6d.

STEPHEN (C. E.)—THE SERVICE OF THE POOR; Being an Inquiry into the Reasons for and against the Establishment of Religious Sisterhoods for Charitable Purposes. By CAROLINE EMILIA STEPHEN. Crown 8vo. 6s. 6d.

STEPHEN.—Works by Sir JAMES FITZJAMES STEPHEN, K.C.S.I., D.C.L. 'A Judge of the High Court of Justice, Queen's Bench Division.
A DIGEST OF THE LAW OF EVIDENCE. Fifth Edition. Crown 8vo. 6s.
A HISTORY OF THE CRIMINAL LAW OF ENGLAND. Three Vols. Demy 8vo. 48s.
A DIGEST OF THE CRIMINAL LAW. (Crimes and Punishments.) Fourth Edition. 8vo. 16s.
A DIGEST OF THE LAW OF CRIMINAL PROCEDURE IN INDICTABLE OFFENCES. By Sir JAMES F. STEPHEN, K.C.S.I., a Judge of the High Court of Justice, Queen's Bench Division, and HERBERT STEPHEN, LL.M, of the Middle Temple, Barrister-at-Law. 8vo. 12s. 6d.
LETTERS ON THE ILBERT BILL. Reprinted from *The Times*. 8vo. 2s.

STEPHEN (J. K.).—INTERNATIONAL LAW AND INTERNATIONAL RELATIONS: an Attempt to Ascertain the Best Method of Discussing the Topics of International Law. By J. K. STEPHEN, B.A., of the Inner Temple, Barrister-at-Law. Crown 8vo. 6s.

STUBBS.—VILLAGE POLITICS. Addresses and Sermons on the Labour Question. By C. W. STUBBS, M.A., Vicar of Granborough, Bucks. Extra fcap. 8vo. 3s. 6d.

THOMPSON.—PUBLIC OPINION AND LORD BEACONSFIELD, 1875-1880. By GEO. CARSLAKE THOMPSON, LL.M., of the Inner Temple, Barrister-at-Law. 2 vols. Demy 8vo. 36s.

THORNTON.—Works by W. T. THORNTON, C.B., Secretary for Public Works in the India Office:—
A PLEA FOR PEASANT PROPRIETORS: With the Outlines of a Plan for their Establishment in Ireland. New Edition, revised. Crown 8vo. 7s. 6d.
INDIAN PUBLIC WORKS AND COGNATE INDIAN TOPICS. With Map of Indian Railways. Crown 8vo. 8s. 6d.

TREVELYAN.—CAWNPORE. By the Right Honourable Sir GEORGE O. TREVELYAN, Bart., M.P., Author of "The Competition Wallah." New Edition. Crown 8vo. 6s.

WALLACE.—BAD TIMES. An Essay on the present Depression of Trade, tracing it to its Sources in enormous Foreign Loans, excessive War Expenditure, the increase of Speculation and of Millionaires, and the Depopulation of the Rural Districts. With suggested Remedies. By ALFRED RUSSEL WALLACE. Crown 8vo. 2s. 6d.

WALKER.—Works by F. A. WALKER, M.A., Ph.D., Professor of Political Economy and History, Yale College.
THE WAGES QUESTION. A Treatise on Wages and the Wages Class. 8vo. 14s.
MONEY. 8vo. 16s.
MONEY IN ITS RELATIONS TO TRADE AND INDUSTRY. Crown 8vo. 7s. 6d.
POLITICAL ECONOMY. Second Edition, Revised. 8vo. 12s. 6d.
LAND AND ITS RENT. Fcap. 8vo. 3s. 6d.
A BRIEF TEXT-BOOK OF POLITICAL ECONOMY. Crown 8vo. 6s. 6d.

WILLIAMS.—FORENSIC FACTS AND FALLACIES. A Popular Consideration of some Legal Points and Principles. By SYDNEY E. WILLIAMS, Barrister-at-Law. Globe 8vo. 4s. 6d.

WORKS CONNECTED WITH THE SCIENCE OR THE HISTORY OF LANGUAGE.

ABBOTT.—A SHAKESPERIAN GRAMMAR: An Attempt to Illustrate some of the Differences between Elizabethan and Modern English. By the Rev. E. A. ABBOTT, D.D., Head Master of the City of London School. New and Enlarged Edition. Extra fcap. 8vo. 6s.

BREYMANN.—A FRENCH GRAMMAR BASED ON PHILOLOGICAL PRINCIPLES. By HERMANN BREYMANN, Ph.D., Professor of Philology in the University of Munich, Lecturer on French Language and Literature in Owens College, Manchester. Extra fcap. 8vo. 4s. 6d.

ELLIS.—PRACTICAL HINTS ON THE QUANTITATIVE PRO-NUNCIATION OF LATIN, FOR THE USE OF CLASSICAL TEACHERS AND LINGUISTS. By A. J. ELLIS, B.A., F.R.S., &c. Extra fcap. 8vo. 4s. 6d.

FASNACHT.—Works by G. EUGÈNE FASNACHT, Author of "Macmillan's Progressive French Course," Editor of "Macmillan's Foreign School Classics," &c.
THE ORGANIC METHOD OF STUDYING LANGUAGES. I. French. Crown 8vo. 3s. 6d.
A SYNTHETIC FRENCH GRAMMAR FOR SCHOOLS. Crown 8vo. 3s. 6d.

FLEAY.—A SHAKESPEARE MANUAL. By the Rev. F. G. FLEAY, M.A., Head Master of Skipton Grammar School. Extra fcap. 8vo. 4s. 6d.

GOODWIN.—Works by W. W. GOODWIN, Professor of Greek Literature in Harvard University.
SYNTAX OF THE GREEK MOODS AND TENSES. New Edition. Crown 8vo. 6s. 6d.
A SCHOOL GREEK GRAMMAR. Crown 8vo. 3s. 6d.
A GREEK GRAMMAR. Crown 8vo. 6s.

GREEK TESTAMENT.—THE NEW TESTAMENT IN THE ORIGINAL GREEK. The Text revised by B. F. WESTCOTT, D.D., Regius Professor of Divinity, and F. J. A. HORT, D.D., Lady Margaret Professor of Divinity, Fellow of Emmanuel College, Cambridge; late Fellows of Trinity College, Cambridge. Two Vols. Crown 8vo. 10s. 6d.
Vol. I. Text.—Vol. II. Introduction and Appendix.
THE NEW TESTAMENT IN THE ORIGINAL GREEK, FOR SCHOOLS. The Text Revised by BROOKE FOSS WESTCOTT, D.D., and FENTON JOHN ANTHONY HORT, D.D. 12mo. cloth. 4s. 6d.; 18mo. roan, red edges, 5s. 6d.

HADLEY.—ESSAYS PHILOLOGICAL AND CRITICAL. Selected from the Papers of JAMES HADLEY, LL.D., Professor of Greek in Yale College, &c. 8vo. 16s.

HALES.—LONGER ENGLISH POEMS. With Notes, Philological and Explanatory, and an Introduction on the Teaching of English. Chiefly for use in Schools. Edited by J. W. HALES, M.A., Professor of English Literature at King's College, London, &c. &c. Eleventh Edition. Extra fcap. 8vo. 4s. 6d.

HELFENSTEIN (JAMES).—A COMPARATIVE GRAMMAR OF THE TEUTONIC LANGUAGES: Being at the same time a Historical Grammar of the English Language, and comprising Gothic, Anglo-Saxon, Early English, Modern English, Icelandic (Old Norse), Danish, Swedish, Old High German, Middle High German, Modern German, Old Saxon, Old Frisian, and Dutch. By JAMES HELFENSTEIN, Ph.D. 8vo. 18s.

MASSON (GUSTAVE).—A COMPENDIOUS DICTIONARY OF THE FRENCH LANGUAGE (French-English and English-French). Adapted from the Dictionaries of Professor ALFRED ELWALL. Followed by a List of the Principal Diverging Derivations, and preceded by Chronological and Historical Tables. By GUSTAVE MASSON, late Assistant-Master and Librarian, Harrow School. New Edition. Crown 8vo. 6s.

MAYOR.—A BIBLIOGRAPHICAL CLUE TO LATIN LITERATURE. Edited after Dr. E. HUBNER. With large Additions by JOHN E. B. MAYOR, M.A., Professor of Latin in the University of Cambridge. Crown 8vo. 10s. 6d.

MORRIS.—Works by the Rev. RICHARD MORRIS, LL.D., President of the Philological Society, Editor of "Specimens of Early English," &c., &c.
HISTORICAL OUTLINES OF ENGLISH ACCIDENCE, comprising Chapters on the History and Development of the Language, and on Word-formation. New Edition. Fcap. 8vo. 6s.
ELEMENTARY LESSONS IN HISTORICAL ENGLISH GRAMMAR, containing Accidence and Word-formation. New Edition. 18mo. 2s. 6d.

OLIPHANT.—Works by T. L. KINGTON OLIPHANT, M.A., of Balliol College, Oxford.
THE OLD AND MIDDLE ENGLISH. A New Edition, revised and greatly enlarged, of "The Sources of Standard English." Extra fcap. 8vo. 9s.
THE NEW ENGLISH. 2 vols. Crown 8vo. 21s.

PHILOLOGY.—THE JOURNAL OF SACRED AND CLASSICAL PHILOLOGY. Four Vols. 8vo. 12s. 6d. each.
THE JOURNAL OF PHILOLOGY. New Series. Edited by JOHN E. B. MAYOR, M.A., and W. ALDIS WRIGHT, M.A. 4s. 6d. (Half-yearly.)
THE AMERICAN JOURNAL OF PHILOLOGY. Edited by BASIL L. GILDERSLEEVE, Professor of Greek in the Johns Hopkins University. 8vo. 4s. 6d. (Quarterly.)

PHRYNICHUS.—THE NEW PHRYNICHUS. Being a Revised Text of *The Ecloga* of the Grammarian *Phrynichus*. With Introductions and Commentary. By W. GUNION RUTHERFORD, M.A., LL.D. of Balliol College Head-Master of Westminster. 8vo. 18s.

ROBY (H. J.)—Works by HENRY JOHN ROBY, M.A., late Fellow of St John's College, Cambridge.
A GRAMMAR OF THE LATIN LANGUAGE, FROM PLAUTUS TO SUETONIUS. In Two Parts. Second Edition. Part I. containing:—Book I. Sounds. Book II. Inflexions. Book III. Word Formation. Appendices. Crown 8vo. 9s. Part II.—Syntax. Prepositions, &c. Crown 8vo. 10s. 6d.
A LATIN GRAMMAR FOR SCHOOLS. Crown 8vo. 5s.

SCHAFF.—THE GREEK TESTAMENT AND THE ENGLISH VERSION, A COMPANION TO. By PHILIP SCHAFF, D.D., President of the American Committee of Revision. With Facsimile Illustrations of MSS. and Standard Editions of the New Testament. Crown 8vo. 12s.

SCHMIDT.—THE RHYTHMIC AND METRIC OF THE CLASSICAL LANGUAGES. To which are added, the Lyric Parts of the "Medea" of Euripides and the "Antigone" of Sophocles; with Rhythmical Scheme and Commentary. By Dr. J. H. SCHMIDT. Translated from the German by J. W. WHITE, D.D. 8vo. 10s. 6d.

TAYLOR.—Works by the Rev. ISAAC TAYLOR, M.A.
ETRUSCAN RESEARCHES. With Woodcuts. 8vo. 14s.
WORDS AND PLACES: or, Etymological Illustrations of History, Ethnology, and Geography. By the Rev. ISAAC TAYLOR. Third Edition, revised and compressed. With Maps. Globe 8vo. 6s.
GREEKS AND GOTHS: a Study of the Runes. 8vo. 9s

VINCENT AND DICKSON.—A HANDBOOK TO MODERN GREEK. By Sir EDGAR VINCENT, K.C.M.G., and T. G. DICKSON, M.A. Second Edition, revised and enlarged. With an Appendix on the Relation of Modern Greek to Classical Greek. By Professor R. C. JEBB. Crown 8vo. 6s.

WHITNEY.—A COMPENDIOUS GERMAN GRAMMAR. By W. D. WHITNEY, Professor of Sanskrit and Instructor in Modern Languages in Yale College. Crown 8vo. 6s.

WHITNEY AND EDGREN.—A COMPENDIOUS GERMAN AND ENGLISH DICTIONARY, with Notation of Correspondences and Brief Etymologies. By Professor W. D. WHITNEY, assisted by A. H. EDGREN. Crown 8vo. 7s. 6d.
The GERMAN-ENGLISH Part may be had separately. Price 5s.

WRIGHT (ALDIS).—THE BIBLE WORD-BOOK: a Glossary of Archaic Words and Phrases in the Authorised Version of the Bible and the Book of Common Prayer. By W. ALDIS WRIGHT, M.A., Fellow and Bursar of Trinity College, Cambridge. Second Edition, revised nd enlarged. Crown 8vo. 7s. 6d.

ZECHARIAH.—THE HEBREW STUDENT'S COMMENTARY ON HEBREW AND LXX. With Excursus on Several Grammatical Subjects. By W. H. LOWE, M.A., Hebrew Lecturer at Christ's College, Cambridge. Demy 8vo. 10s. 6d.

THE GOLDEN TREASURY SERIES.

UNIFORMLY printed in 18mo, with Vignette Titles by Sir J. E. MILLAIS, T. WOOLNER, W. HOLMAN HUNT, Sir NOEL PATON, ARTHUR HUGHES, &c. Engraved on Steel by JEENS. Bound in extra cloth, 4s. 6d. each volume.

THE GOLDEN TREASURY OF THE BEST SONGS AND LYRICAL POEMS IN THE ENGLISH LANGUAGE. Selected and arranged, with Notes, by Professor FRANCIS TURNER PALGRAVE.

THE CHILDREN'S GARLAND FROM THE BEST POETS. Selected and arranged by COVENTRY PATMORE.

THE BOOK OF PRAISE. From the best English Hymn Writers. Selected and arranged by ROUNDELL, EARL OF SELBORNE.

THE FAIRY BOOK; the Best Popular Fairy Stories. Selected and rendered anew by the Author of "JOHN HALIFAX, GENTLEMAN."

THE BALLAD BOOK. A Selection of the Choicest British Ballads. Edited by WILLIAM ALLINGHAM.

THE JEST BOOK. The Choicest Anecdotes and Sayings. Selected and arranged by MARK LEMON.

BACON'S ESSAYS AND COLOURS OF GOOD AND EVIL. With Notes and Glossarial Index. By W. ALDIS WRIGHT, M.A.

THE PILGRIM'S PROGRESS from this World to that which is to come. By JOHN BUNYAN.

THE SUNDAY BOOK OF POETRY FOR THE YOUNG. Selected and arranged by C. F. ALEXANDER.

A BOOK OF GOLDEN DEEDS of All Times and All Countries. Gathered and Narrated Anew. By the Author of "THE HEIR OF REDCLYFFE."

THE ADVENTURES OF ROBINSON CRUSOE. Edited, from the Original Edition, by J. W. CLARK, M.A.

THE REPUBLIC OF PLATO, TRANSLATED INTO ENGLISH, with Notes by J. LL. DAVIES, M.A., and D. J. VAUGHAN, M.A.

THE SONG BOOK. Words and Tunes from the best Poets and Musicians. Selected and arranged by JOHN HULLAH.

LA LYRE FRANÇAISE. Selected and arranged, with Notes, by GUSTAVE MASSON. French Master in Harrow School.

TOM BROWN'S SCHOOL DAYS. By AN OLD BOY.

A BOOK OF WORTHIES. Gathered from the Old Histories and written anew by the Author of "THE HEIR OF REDCLYFFE."

GUESSES AT TRUTH. By Two BROTHERS. *New Edition.*

THE CAVALIER AND HIS LADY. Selections from the Works of the First Duke and Duchess of Newcastle. With an Introductory Essay by EDWARD JENKINS, Author of "Ginx's Baby," &c.

SCOTCH SONG. A Selection of the Choicest Lyrics of Scotland. Compiled and arranged, with brief Notes, by MARY CARLYLE AITKEN.

DEUTSCHE LYRIK: The Golden Treasury of the best German Lyrical Poems. Selected and arranged, by Dr. BUCHHEIM.

HERRICK: Selections from the Lyrical Poems. Arranged, with Notes, by F. T. PALGRAVE.

POEMS OF PLACES. Edited by H. W. LONGFELLOW. England and Wales, Two Vols.

MATTHEW ARNOLD'S SELECTED POEMS.

THE STORY OF THE CHRISTIANS AND MOORS IN SPAIN. By C. M. YONGE, Author of the "Heir of Redclyffe"

CHARLES LAMB'S TALES FROM SHAKESPEARE.— Edited by the Rev. ALFRED AINGER, M.A.

A BOOK OF GOLDEN THOUGHTS. By HENRY ATTWELL.

POEMS OF WORDSWORTH. Chosen and Edited, with Preface by MATTHEW ARNOLD. (Also a Large Paper Edition. Crown 8vo. 9s.)

SHAKESPEARE'S SONNETS. Edited by F. T. PALGRAVE.

POEMS FROM SHELLEY. Selected and arranged by STOPFORD A. BROOKE. M.A. (Also a Large Paper Edition. Crown 8vo. 12s 6d.)

ESSAYS OF JOSEPH ADDISON. Chosen and Edited by JOHN RICHARD GREEN, M.A., LL.D.

POETRY OF BYRON. Chosen and arranged by MATTHEW ARNOLD. (Also a Large Paper Edition. Crown 8vo. 9s.)

SELECTIONS FROM THE WRITINGS OF WALTER SAVAGE LANDOR.—Arranged and Edited by SIDNEY COLVIN.

SIR THOMAS BROWNE'S RELIGIO MEDICI; Letter to a Friend, &c., and Christian Morals. Edited by W. A GREENHILL, M.D.

THE SPEECHES AND TABLE-TALK OF THE PROPHET MOHAMMAD.—Chosen and Translated, with an Introduction and Notes, by STANLEY LANE-POOLE.

SELECTIONS FROM COWPER'S POEMS.—With an Introduction by Mrs. OLIPHANT.

LETTERS OF WILLIAM COWPER.—Edited, with Introduction. By the Rev. W. BENHAM, B.D.

THE POETICAL WORKS OF JOHN KEATS.—Reprinted from the Original Editions, with Notes. By FRANCIS TURNER PALGRAVE.

LYRICAL POEMS. By LORD TENNYSON. Selected and Annotated by FRANCIS TURNER PALGRAVE.

IN MEMORIAM. By LORD TENNYSON, Poet Laureate.

*** Large Paper Edition. 8vo. 9s.

THE TRIAL AND DEATH OF SOCRATES. Being the Euthyphron, Apology, Crito, and Phaedo of Plato. Translated into English by F. J. CHURCH.

PLATO. PHÆDRUS, LYSIS, AND PROTAGORAS. Translated by Rev. JOSIAH WRIGHT, M.A.

*** *Other Volumes to follow.*

A MAGAZINE FOR EVERY HOUSEHOLD.

"A Magazine which has no rival in England."—*The Times.*

The *St. James's Gazette* says:—"This volume contains a vast variety of good reading, interspersed with a great number of illustrations of a quality for which this periodical has become famous. . . . The magazine is a delightful example of good typography and sound engraving."

The *Glasgow Herald* says:—"It is a mine of literature and art."

The *Scotsman* says:—"It is the most beautiful of all magazines."

The *Saturday Review* says:—It is as pretty a book for presentation as could be desired."

The English Illustrated Magazine.

(PROFUSELY ILLUSTRATED)

Single Numbers, price 6d. ; Double Number, 1s.

THE ENGLISH ILLUSTRATED MAGAZINE is designed for the entertainment of the home, and for the instruction and amusement of young and old, and it is conducted in the belief that every section of its readers, in whatever direction their tastes and interests may tend, are prepared to demand and to appreciate the best that can be offered to them.

The Volume for 1888 is now ready, price 8s. It consists of 832 closely-printed pages, and contains nearly 500 Woodcut Illustrations of various sizes, bound in Extra Cloth, Coloured Edges.

Among the Chief Contents of the Volume are the following Complete Stories and Serials :—

Coaching Days and Coaching Ways. By W. O. TRISTRAM. With Illustrations by H. RAILTON and HUGH THOMSON.	**The Mediation of Ralph Hardelot.** By Prof. W. MINTO.
The Story of Jael. By the Author of "Mehalah."	**That Girl in Black.** By Mrs. MOLESWORTH.
Lil: a Liverpool Child. By AGNES C. MAITLAND.	**Glimpses of Old English Homes.** By ELIZABETH BALCH.
The Patagonia. By HENRY JAMES.	**Pagodas, Aurioles, and Umbrellas.** By C. F. GORDON CUMMING.
Family Portraits. By S. J. WEYMAN.	**The Magic Fan.** By JOHN STRANGE WINTER.

And numerous shorter Stories, Papers, and Essays, by well-known Writers, with Illustrations by Eminent Artists.

MACMILLAN & CO., LONDON.

www.ingramcontent.com/pod-product-compliance
Lightning Source LLC
Chambersburg PA
CBHW020141170426
43199CB00010B/841